WHY?

Because You Are Anointed!

WHY?

Because You Are Anointed!

T.D. Jakes

DESTINY IMAGE® PUBLISHERS, INC.
P.O. Box 310, Shippensburg, PA 17257-0310

"Speaking to the Purposes of God for this Generation and for the Generations to Come."

This book and all other Destiny Image, Revival Press, Mercy Place, Fresh Bread, Destiny Image Fiction, and Treasure House books are available at Christian bookstores and distributors worldwide.

For a U.S. bookstore nearest you, call:
1-800-722-6774.

For more information on foreign distributors, call:
717-532-3040.

Or reach us on the Internet: www.destinyimage.com.

ISBN 10: 0-7684-2643-X
ISBN 13: 978-0-7684-2643-4

For Worldwide Distribution, Printed in the U.S.A.

15 16 17 / 21 20 19

Previously Published by Pneuma Life Publishing
ISBN 1-56229-434-2; Copyright © 1994 by T.D. Jakes.

Table of Contents

Foreword

    I cannot think of a greater living example of the consistent ability to draw on the anointing of the Lord. T.D. Jakes is man without equal. There is much we can all learn from his words, his spirit and his passion in delivering the word of the Lord. Just watching him is a wonder in itself. The presence of the Lord flows so freely from him as he teaches. He is simple, clear, and honest in his delivery; sometimes urgent, sometimes gentle, but always accurate and penetrating. He is a man whose inner focus is on the Lord Himself. Even in his most emotional presentation, you can also see the rest and peace in his eyes. The Holy Spirit will always move freely through those who have no other desire than to give the word of the Lord to hungry people. And make no mistake about it, God has much to say to His people. He has much He wants to communicate to the world around us. There is much to learn from the Bishop's words, but also his method, his passion, and his love of the Lord Jesus Himself.

I first met the Bishop at a small conference in the Pocono Mountains where he was ministering. That was just before he wrote *Woman, Thou Art Loosed.* We literally walked into each other that fateful afternoon in the basement area of the conference center where vendors were displaying their products. The moment I touched him I prophesied about a book churning in his heart. A few weeks later he called me and the rest, as they say, is history.

There are three criteria we use when determining the possibility of publishing a new author. We look at the person, his message, and his ministry. In the Bishop's case, all three were intricately wrapped with integrity, gentleness, and truth. We are proud to offer this work to the world. He is a man who has allowed the Lord to mold him into a vessel He can use to change the lives of millions around the world. We are grateful to be a part of God's plan for the life of Bishop T.D. Jakes.

Don Nori, Publisher
Destiny Image Publishers

Introduction

How long, O Lord, must I call for help, but you do not listen? Or cry to you, "Violence!" but you do not save? Why do you make me look at injustice? Why do you tolerate wrong? Destruction and violence are before me; there is strife, and conflict abounds. Therefore the law is paralyzed, and justice never prevails. The wicked hem in the righteous, so that justice is perverted.... Your eyes are too pure to look on evil; you cannot tolerate wrong. Why then do you tolerate the treacherous? Why are you silent while the wicked swallow up those more righteous than themselves? (Habakkuk 1:2-4,13 NIV)

Have you been waiting on God for an answer?

Have you been asking God questions about your life and the society in which we live? Why so much heartache, so much pain? Have you, like the prophet Habakkuk, become perplexed, distraught, saddened, grieved, and even angered at the injustices of today? What about the plight of the poor, the pain of the oppressed, the continual wickedness of mankind, and the hypocrisy and complacency of the Church? Have you cried in the midnight hour and asked God, "How long?" Have you thought, like Habakkuk, that maybe God just was not listening?

Are there problems in your life left unresolved, questions unanswered? Have you considered entering into the courtroom of the kingdom of God to ask, "God, Your Honor, why? What's going on? What is the purpose? What's happening in my life?"

"Lord, I don't mean to intrude on Your busy schedule, but if You would, please just reveal to me the method to this madness. Your master plan must be a divine strategy." God says, "Wait on Me, I'm going to answer you. I'm going to speak to you. I'm going to talk to you. I'm going to show you My glory and My power."

Why is not necessarily a rebellious attempt to question God's authority. Why is just wanting to understand and be at one with God's reasoning. Why are the children of Israel knowing the acts of God but Moses knowing the ways (His heart and reasoning) of God. Why is a desire for a divine impartation and revelation from God, wanting His mind to be in you, which is the mind of Christ.

Why is saying, "God, I want to be a clone of Your wisdom. I want to draw from Your spiritual and intellectual resources until Your thoughts become my thoughts, and Your ways become my ways, and Your ideas become my ideas. I want a supernatural exchange."

"God, I'm not questioning Your right or ability to rule or govern, but show me the strategy. Show me Your plan and purpose for my life. Let me see the blueprint before the building is built. Let me see the plan before the product is manufactured. I just want to know what I shall be when I get through crying, suffering, and laboring in turmoil and confusion. Every now and then, tell me and remind me how it's going to end!"

You don't feel a great amount of emotional intensity when you read the word why or speak the word why. But when a sincere, heartfelt, passion-filled why comes out of one's heart, it is often the consequence of a certain amount of bewilderment and perplexity. It comes from one who has become distraught, despondent, and discouraged. One that says, "I've reached the end of my rope. I've come to the end of my reasoning and can't understand why. Why must I suffer? Why must I cry? Why must I keep reaching out to people who hurt me? Why am I misunderstood? Why do I keep going through the same things again and again and again? Why do I keep going through periods of prolonged confusion? I'm not saying I'm going to quit or I'm going to backslide. I'm not getting ready to go out, get drunk, throw in the towel, surrender to the temptation and the pressure of satan or the lust of the world. But God, I'm on my knees and I just want to know why?

14

"Why do the wicked seem to prosper over the righteous? Why do the hypocrites seem to get all the blessings, and the real saints go without? Why are the anointed persecuted? Why does there seem to be no justice? Why does the vision tarry? This is an emergency! It's an SOS. It's a 911. Lord, I need a breakthrough right now; not tomorrow, not next week, next month, or next year. Lord, I need it now!"

Why is the blessing delayed? Why must I wait? Why do the heathens rage? Great God! Why is there so much hoopla going on in my life? Why do the people imagine vain things? They just make up things, or come up with strange things. Am I in the right place at the wrong time, or the wrong place at the right time? Lord, what's up? Why are the minds of men coming up with all of these illusions to perplex me and disturb me? Why is everybody tripping on me? Why do vain things, empty things, lifeless things, and dead things keep bombarding my thinking and my life? Why, why, why, why, why, why?

Why have the kings of the earth (men and women of position, prestige, and authority) set themselves against me? Could it just be because I am anointed?

15

You do know that anointed folks go through more than everybody else! I used to have the wrong notion that when you are really anointed, you no longer have problems or rough times. But you show me anybody who's really Holy Ghost, knee-jerking, tongue-talking, casting-out-demons, laying-hands-on-the-sick, miracle-working, world-changing, mind-transforming, mind-boggling, head-straightening anointed, and I'll show you somebody who cried in the middle of the night and suffered all night long, wondering where is God. "I looked on the right and you were not there. I looked on the left and you were not there." Anybody who's really anointed has suffered some things, has gone without, has been lonely, has agonized, has had to press through, and has crawled a mile or two. But, my friends, I have to confess that through it all I, like the anointed ones, have learned to trust in Jesus. Through it all, I've learned to trust in God. Though He slay me, yet will I praise Him. Why? It's the anointing!

Perhaps you've been bewildered, confused, or discouraged while waiting on God. Have you wondered why your vision tarries or when things are going to start looking up? Why is it taking so long for morning to come? Why is my change not coming forth? If you've been totally preoccupied, consumed, over-whelmed, and overcome with why? and still have no answers, my beloved brothers and sisters, I can only tell you what God told me some time ago: "Get Ready! Get Ready! Get Ready! Get Ready! Get Ready! Get Ready!"

Chapter 1
Why?

Why?

Why do the heathen rage, and the people imagine a vain thing? The kings of the earth set themselves, and the rulers take counsel together, against the Lord, and against His anointed... (Psalm 2:1-2).

Why? The word why is a request of a student, not merely for an answer, but for the understanding of the procedure that leads to an answer. It is not just a request saying, "Give me the bottom line answer." Why is the student saying, "Explain the dynamics of the issue, the situation, or the problem until I fully understand in absolute and complete detail the process that leads me to the solution." The American Dictionary defines *why* this way: For what purpose, reason, or cause, with what intention, justification or motive, the cause or intention underlying a given action or situation, a difficult problem or question. *Why:* Used to express mild indignation, surprise or impatience.

Why? Every mother will tell you that children go through a time of asking why. No matter how many answers you give them, they keep asking, "Why?"

"Why is it light outside, Daddy?" "Because the sun is shining, son." "Why is the sun shining?" "Because God wanted the sun to shine." "Why did God want the sun to shine?" "Because we need sunlight." "Why do we need sunlight? Why?" "Because sunlight helps us to grow." "Why does it help us grow?"

After this line of questioning, you become exasperated, exhausted, and frustrated. You finally say, "Why do you keep saying, why? Why do you keep asking me the same thing over and over again? I've

Why?

given you an answer, but you just keep asking me 'why?'"

Why does not merely say "give me an answer." It's a demand, an inquiry, a request that you talk with me, that you dialogue with me until I understand your thought process. It says, "Communicate with me until I understand your wisdom, until I know how to deduce for myself and determine in my mind the things that you have deciphered in your maturity. I know that I may appear to be inferior and my intellect may be less developed than yours, but explain the situation and break it down to my level of understanding that I might be able to determine the matter for myself. That way, when you're not around, I can equate and come to a solution or conclusion on my own without the help of others. I need to think in a decisive manner for myself that I may learn to be independent."

Why? My father said something to me before he passed away. He was on his deathbed and his words changed my life. He was fading away, in front of me, as a young man in his early forties. While I sat at his bedside, my father's words were very simple, yet profound. He said, "Son, I want you to

23

know something. By the time I figured out what life was really all about, it was time to go." That bothered me. That troubled me. That angered me. It really disturbed me.

I thought, "I don't want to spend all of my life trying to figure out what life's really all about, and by the time I finally realize what's actually going on, it's time to go." From that moment, I started playing beat-the-clock. "God, I want to know why? I want to know now, not when I'm an old man or on my deathbed. I want to be able to decipher, to determine and to realize purpose, to understand what is the true meaning for my existence. Away with the trivialities, the small stuff, the surface stuff, and the superficial issues. I want to know the real deal; the intrinsic nature of the thing. Give me the divine philosophy, the heavenly strategy, and the majestic plan. I want to know what it's really all about. Please God, answer the why of the matter."

English novelist Charles Dickens wrote in his famous book, *A Tale of Two Cities*, "Life is a tale told by a fool." He said not to ask why, because there is no answer. Life, according to Dickens, is just a bombardment of separated incidents that have no harmony, relativity, or relationship with one another. It's just this, that, and the other. In life there is no formation, no conclusion, no answer—just a wild man telling a strange story that has no ending, solution, or equation. Life is sporadic, out of control, wild, crazy, and all mixed up. Don't try to figure it out. Just leave it where it is. Don't worry about it. Just lay it down to the side. Don't try to understand anything about what life is really all about.

But Dickens was wrong. The question that needs to be answered is, "Why are all the fatalists and misguided doomsayers of the world wrong?" It is this question of the anointed person's unanswered dilemma of joy and pain, suffering and comfort, tragedy and triumph, which this book seeks to address.

Having a Divine Perspective

Charles Dickens was wrong in his assessment of life. He sought to draw a conclusion without acknowledging and inquiring from the One who has given life to all men. God is the Creator of man and all living things. The biblical perspective of life is not one of unfulfilled dreams or unanswered prayers. The biblical, godly perspective of life is one of insight, direction, hope, fulfilled dreams and visions. Just because the vision tarries doesn't mean God has changed His mind or given up on you. It could very well mean that the timing or the situation is not right for God to get the ultimate glory and benefit out of your trusting in Him. Hold on to faith even in the midst of the battle.

The vision could be delayed because God knows you're not mature enough to handle the success. Perhaps it will result in a new and fresh anointing you've been seeking. Maybe the vision tarries because, even though you're saved, baptized with the Holy Ghost, and a little bit sanctified, your heavenly Father knows there's a part of that old sinful man that hasn't quite died. But, I'll tell you as a living witness, if you hold on and wait a little while longer, your change is going to come. God will come through in the end.

The vision could be delayed because God knows you're not mature enough to handle the success.

Stand like Shadrach, Meshach, and Abednego. Do not bow to the temptation of man's agenda or to ungodly persuasion. Do not try to keep up with the Joneses or bow to selfish ambition and self-promotion. Do not bow to the spirit of anxiousness and impatience. Continue to walk by faith and not by sight, knowing God is able to do more abundantly and exceedingly than all you could ask or think (see Ephesians 3:20). God is able to finish that good work He began in you when you first gave your life to Him. If you do these things and maintain the faith, regardless of the external circumstances, in time you will come out as pure gold, a vessel of honor.

Before we begin our journey into the realm of truth and Spirit, please allow me to say that I do not propose that this one book will answer all the whys that preoccupy your thoughts and mind. What I endeavor to do is present you with some basic biblical principles, some precious spiritual jewels that, if acted on, will give you better insight into the heart of your heavenly Father. He desires for us to ask for direction for our lives.

Remember, those who love God with all that is in them and who hold fast to their trust in the Father, can enjoy the saying:

Good things truly do come to those who wait. The determining factor is who you're waiting on. God says in Ecclesiastes 3:1, "There is a purpose and a time for all things." There is reason for man's existence. There is some good working out of the matter. There is some logic to the development and a major strategy that causes all of these broken pieces to fit together. If we relate to God like a student to a teacher and ask why long enough, and are persistent enough, we will begin to understand what the why is all about.

Why?

Thoughts and Reflections

_____

WHY? BECAUSE YOU ARE ANOINTED!

_____
_____
_____
_____
_____
_____
_____
_____
_____
_____
_____
_____
_____
_____
_____
_____
_____
_____
_____
_____
_____
_____
_____

Why?

_____

_____

_____

_____

_____

_____

_____

_____

_____

_____

_____

_____

_____

_____

_____

_____

_____

_____

_____

_____

_____

_____

_____

_____ ◆

Chapter 2
Seek and Ye Shall Find

Seek and Ye Shall Find

I was taught not to ask God, "Why?" I was taught that true Christians never ask God why. It was considered a breech of our faith to ask God why. If you really believe God, you just completely accept everything that comes your way without asking God anything pertaining to its reason for happening: It's as if God gets insulted, mad, or feels like you're questioning His authority when you ask Him why? Others feel that if you ask why, God is intimidated with your quest for knowledge or that you might ask Him something that He cannot answer or that you might offend or hinder God's ability to be omniscient. For whatever the reason, you just don't ask Almighty God, why?

However, the Bible says, "If any of you lack wisdom, let him ask of God, that giveth to all men liberally, and upbraideth not" (James 1:5). God said, "Come to Me and ask Me why." He said, "I'm not afraid of your questions. I'm not afraid of you." God is not insecure in His sovereignty. He's not envious of man or afraid that His position, power, or authority is going to be jeopardized by you or anybody else knowing too much. I don't care how many times you have to ask Him. He says ask of Him who giveth freely as He wills. God said, "When you are confused, your mind is perplexed, your heart is troubled, and you don't know what-in-the-world to do, come to Me and ask Me. Lay all the cards down on the table. Say, this is happening and that is happening. There's trouble here and there's trouble there. There's trouble everywhere. I've been serving You all I know how, and it looks like things are getting worse instead of better. God, why?" God says He can handle it. Bring it to Him. "I'm able," says God, "to share with you the kind of truth that transforms." God says, "Cry out to Me; inquire of Me. Knock and the door shall be opened, seek and ye shall find."

God shares with us truth
that transforms.

Faith in God,
the Key to Answered Prayers

God says when you've searched for Him
with your whole heart (your entire being),
then you will find Him. If we are serious
about hearing from God, we're going to have
to exercise the kind of faith that is strong
and persistent just like the woman in Jesus'
parable about the unjust judge.

*And he spake a parable unto them to
this end, that men ought always to
pray, and not to faint; Saying, There
was in a city a judge, which feared
not God, neither regarded man: And
there was a widow in that city; and
she came unto him, saying, Avenge
me of mine adversary. And he would
not for awhile: but afterward he said
within himself, Though I fear not God,
nor regard man; Yet because this
widow troubleth me, I will avenge her,
lest by her continual coming She*

37

weary me. And the Lord said, Hear what the unjust judge saith. And shall not God avenge his own elect, which cry day and night unto him, though he bear long with them? I tell you he will avenge them speedily. Nevertheless when the Son of man cometh shall he find faith on the earth? (Luke 18:1-8).

The judge did not want to hear the woman's plea for justice, but the woman pressed him so hard and so long that he granted the woman's request. The judge did this not because he felt sorry for her or had compassion on her, but the judge granted her petition simply because the lady literally "got on his nerves." The widow, realizing the judge's reluctance and refusal to hear her, could have lost hope, lost faith, and simply given up. But the woman was persistent, and her persistence was actually fueled and empowered by her faith; a faith that declares, "I don't care how long it takes; I don't care what I have to suffer or what pain I must endure; I don't care who doesn't agree with me or doesn't like me for believing God; I know that if I keep on keeping on, one day, sooner or later, my change is going to come and I will see the salvation of the Lord."

Regardless of the excesses and some erroneous teachings that have been associated with the "Word of Faith" and charismatic movements, Christians must forever remember and be mindful of the fact that the Word of God declares that anything in our life that is not rooted in or brought about by faith in the Almighty, is sin. For, without faith it is impossible to please God. The just (righteous men and women of God) shall and must live by faith. Faith for the believer is what gasoline is for an automobile; it's what electricity is for lights and high-powered appliances. It (faith in God and confidence in self) is what fuels our lives and gives motivation, inspiration, and eternal hope for our existence.

As the motivational and inspirational speaker Les Brown says about faith in God and in self: "Within you lies the power to seize the hour and live your dreams. Faith is the oil that takes the friction out of living. Faith will enable you to turn liabilities into assets and stumbling blocks into stepping stones. When you begin to have faith, your load will get heavy but your knees won't buckle, you'll get knocked down but you won't get knocked out. You've got to have faith if you are going to make it in life. You must believe in yourself and in a power greater than yourself, and do your best and don't worry about the rest. You must maintain faith and work as if everything depended on you, and pray as if everything depended on God."

Please, let me be clear on what faith is, so that you make no mistakes about what I'm talking about. I'm not talking about some kind of feel-good confession rooted in humanism, saying, "I'm okay, you're okay." Nor am I referring to some kind of manipulation of Scripture to formulate my recipe for success. That's a form of charismatic witchcraft and I don't associate with witches. No! When I say, "Faith," I'm talking about complete, absolute, uncompromising trust in God. It is a faith that knows my successes in life are not because of some great wonderful ability of my own, but my help comes from the Lord. For He, the Lord God Almighty, enables me to do His good will and all things for His good pleasure.

It is God who works all things and does all things together for our good. In accordance with His calling on our lives and His overall purpose for humankind, He does these things (trials as well as blessings) as prerequisites of our love for Him. Love directed toward God is reflected and expressed by our obedience to His Word and submission to His commands (see 1 John 5:2-3). We must know that the supreme principle of faith is the product of God's love toward us. "Faith worketh by love" (Galatians 5:6).

God does all things together for our good.

We often trust only people we know love us, people in whom we are assured have our best interest at heart. With agape love, the recipient's welfare is always the giver's number one concern. Knowing this makes it easier to trust the heavenly Father, the One who loved you while you were yet a sinner, unworthy of love. Having promised that He will never leave or forsake us, no matter how difficult the circumstances, or how severe the situation, we are not without hope. Our hope makes us not ashamed "because the love of God is shed abroad in our hearts by the Holy Ghost which is given unto us" (Romans 5:5). Faith worketh by love.

Patience and Waiting on God

The problem with most Christians is that we are far too impatient. If God doesn't speak in the first five minutes of our prayer time, we get up, shake ourselves off, and concede that God is not talking today. We no longer have the kind of tenacity, diligence, and persistence like the saints of old. Those saints of bygone days would get on their faces before God and grab hold of the horns of the altar and refuse to let go until they received a sure word from God. Unlike those precious men and women of God, we have become the "microwave" generation. We want everything overnight, even Christian maturity. We want whatever is quick, fast, and in a hurry. We've deleted, erased, and totally obliterated from our Bibles, and our thoughts, those passages of Scripture that command us to wait on God during turbulent, troubling, and unsure times.

> *"My brethren, count it all joy when ye fall into divers temptation; knowing this, that the trying of your faith worketh patience. But let patience have her perfect work, that ye may be perfect and entire, wanting nothing"* (James 1:2-4).

You might ask me, "Bishop, why (there's that why again) does it often take God so long to answer our prayers?" We put a petition, request, or question before God on a Monday, and it might be the next week or next month before God gives a reply. This tests our faith in order to see if we will continue to serve God, even if He delays His reply. If God decides to prolong an answer or provision for our needs, are we willing and secure enough in His sovereignty to trust and wait on Him, regardless of how bleak the situation may look? My brothers and sisters, we have to let patience have its perfect (complete, absolute, to full maturity) work.

God's reply to the nagging questions and complex issues that preoccupy our thoughts is, "I may not answer you right away, but go ahead and question why, and wait on Me."

"Wait on Me."

"But they that wait upon the Lord shall renew their strength, they shall mount up on wings like eagles; they shall run and not be weary, and they shall walk and not faint"

(Isaiah 40:31). What are you waiting for? I'm waiting for an answer. Does your vision tarry? Wait for it. Be diligent. Don't become weary in well doing: for in due season you shall reap the reward of your request, your petition, your labor, and the answers to your whys if you faint not (Galatians 6:9).

Has God told you that He has destined you for a certain thing? Has God given you a vision of ministry? Has He promised you a particular blessing? Maybe you're single and God has assured you that you'll be married at an appointed time. But it seems as if the mate that God has fitted for your specific needs is nowhere in sight.

If any of these predicaments are your present experience, I remind you of what God told His prophet Habakkuk. At a time when the prophet was despondent because of what he had seen and experienced, God said, "Write the vision, and make it plain upon tables, that he [you] may run that readeth it to pursue it and fulfill it. For the vision is yet for an appointed time, but at the end it shall speak, and not lie: though it tarry, wait for it; because it will surely come, it will not delay" (Habakkuk 2:2,3).

If God has spoken to you about your life and has shown you a glorious end to the matter, wait on it. If, in your waiting, you exercise faith, prayer, and patience, the vision shall surely come to pass. The Lord your God is not a man that He should lie nor the Son of Man that He should repent. God says, "I know the thoughts that I think toward you...thoughts of peace, and not of evil, to give you an expected end. Then shall ye call upon me, and ye shall go and pray unto me, and I will hearken unto you. And ye shall seek me, and find me, when ye shall search for me with all your heart. And I will be found of you...and I will turn away your captivity" (Jeremiah 29:11-14a).

Tribulations Worketh Patience

Therefore being justified by faith, we have peace with God through our Lord Jesus Christ: By whom also we have access by faith into this grace wherein we stand, and rejoice in hope of the glory of God. And not only so, but we glory in tribulations also: knowing that tribulation worketh patience (Romans 5:1-3).

Patience, contrary to popular belief, is not the same as waiting. Waiting is a passive posture but patience is an active principle. Waiting, by itself, is by no means a guarantee of receiving the promise God has for your life. If that were the case, the five virgins in the Bible, caught without oil in their lamps, would have been ready at the Lord's coming.

Patience is not the same as waiting.

Also, the Hebrews who came out of Egypt would have entered the Promised Land. No! Patience is not just "waiting on God." Patience is based on the scriptural principle of persistence and perseverance (steadfastness in delay). Patience also does not come by prayer alone. As a matter of fact, a prayer for patience is only an acknowledgment of your lack of it and does not mean God will grant your request through a supernatural gift. No! My brother and sister, I wish it was that easy. As a matter of fact, when you ask

God for patience, you only get it as a by-product of something else that the Lord sends your way. Are you curious to know what that something else is? (I know you are!) It is tribulation.

Tribulation. There is absolutely no other God-given way to grow in the fruit of patience. Trib-u-la-tion. The word even sounds funny and undesirable, but it's a necessary element of Christian perfection and a primary prerequisite in receiving the promises of God.

Tribulation. What is it? What does it mean? Is it affliction? Does it mean I'm going to have to suffer? Yes!

Tribulation means all of these and many other undesirable and unwelcome things that I will discuss in a later chapter. But without exercising patience we will not be able to receive the full counsel of the Lord, nor will we see the vision of God in our lives come to pass. There will be no patience without tribulation.

> *There is no patience without tribulation.*

Many times we pray for things, but we don't recognize or understand the answer to our prayers. Remember, in all things God has a divine process and order by which He operates everything on the earth.

We ask for strength, and God sends us difficult situations to make us strong. We pray for wisdom, and God provides us with problems that provoke us to come up with solutions and develop wisdom. We ask for prosperity, and God gives us strength to work and wisdom to invent. We ask for a favor, and God gives us responsibility. A large percentage of our success is the result of our eating the bread of adversity and drinking the bitter waters of affliction.

"The genius of success is to be able to see the good that hides in every situation. As a pessimist sees obstacles in his opportunities, so an optimist sees opportunities in his obstacles." Tribulation worketh patience.

Thoughts and Reflections

_____

_____

_____

_____

_____

_____

_____

_____

_____

_____

_____

_____

_____

_____

_____

_____

_____

_____

_____

_____

_____

_____

Seek and Ye Shall Find

_____

_____

_____

_____

_____

_____

_____

_____

_____

_____

_____

_____

_____

_____

_____

_____

_____

_____

_____

_____

_____

_____

Chapter 3
God's University—School of the Spirit

God's University—School
of the Spirit

A ny teacher will tell you that education begins not with lectures or speeches, but with interaction with the pupil. The classes are not really good until the teacher has sufficiently stimulated the students to the point where they begin to ask questions about the subject being studied. With hands raised, they ask the teacher, why? Then the explanation process begins. Before you know it, you have a serious dialogue going on, all centered around the inquisition, why? As the teacher explains, she establishes a relationship with the student. The teacher knows she has the student in the palm of her hands. If she can get you to ask a question, she has motivated you. When you ask why, you're saying, "I'm interested in what you're doing." At that precise moment, the teacher has engaged you (the student) not only in the education process, but in the actual learning experience.

Teachers who successfully continue in the educating process not only must establish a dialogue with the student, but also must adequately and competently answer complex, difficult, and perplexing questions in the minds of students. The student's line of questioning, from that point, begins to convey a message that says, "I respect your ability as a teacher to be able to give me answers." At this stage in the educational process, trust begins. If the teacher has proven continually that he or she has the student's personal, as well as academic, interest in mind, the learning process advances to the pivotal and the most warranted stage referred to as discipleship.

From that point on, the student communicates to the teacher that through their relationship he wants an exchange. Not only an exchange of answers, but for the teacher to teach him how to reason like a teacher. Therefore, this exchange will enable the student to become a teacher and ultimately teach other people. This is what God really desires and wishes to share with us as disciples of Christ.

> *The student becomes*
> *the teacher.*

God desires all His children to have intimate dialogues with Him, like He had with Adam and Eve before the fall of man. God, our heavenly Father, still seeks to walk with us in the cool of the day. Contrary to erroneous beliefs, God has always sought to communicate with His most blessed and highest earthly creation—mankind. God wants to communicate with us, which is one of the primary reasons He sent the Holy Spirit to commune with us: so that we might learn something of His ways and purposes. The Scripture declares that "Ye need not that any man teach you: but as the same anointing teacheth you of all things, and is truth, and is no lie, and even as it hath taught you, ye shall abide in him" (1 John 2:27).

Just as college professors relate to students, God, by His Spirit, wants to have the same exchange with us. God's desire is to be with us, to work with us, to shape and mold us, to convene and plan with us, and to deal with us until we get to the point that we grow up from being students and become teachers ourselves. "That we henceforth be no more children, tossed to and fro, and carried about with every wind of doctrine, by the sleight of men, and cunning craftiness, whereby they lie in wait to deceive. But speaking the truth in love, may grow up into him in all things, which is the head, even Christ" (Ephesians 4:14,15). Teachers are able to impart wisdom to potential students and wisdom one to another, thus the *School of the Spirit.*

Teacher's Pet

There's no way that you can be the kind of student that goes into overtime and not become the teacher's pet. Remember seeing them in school? They were those students who always were in the teacher's face, and the teacher just loved them. They always asked why, as if everything the teacher

discussed was so interesting. You were probably like me, always so bored and so sick of
them, you wanted to hit them in the head
with an apple. They just kept asking, why?
and the teacher seemed to enjoy them so
much. They had established that teacher-to-
student, student-to-teacher relationship.
God says, "Don't sit in My class and be reluc-
tant to ask questions. I'm the Master
Teacher, the Good Master Teacher." God
says, "If you really want to know, ask Me,
and I will give you the heathen for an inheritance...." (Psalm 2:8). If you really want to
get something going with Me, start draining
from the milk of My wisdom, start pulling
from Me. Ask and it shall be given; knock,
and the door shall be open unto you; seek,
and ye shall find" (Matthew 7:7).

> *If you really want to know
> Me, ask Me.*

God wants us to be inquisitive. He's tired
of His children being passive and just accept-
ing everything that comes into our lives. He
wants us to question Him that we may find
clarity and find effective solutions to the

problems confronting us day-in and day-out. He wants you to take a stand and start asking why? He's tired of us lying down and saying, 'This is the way it's got to be. I don't think there's any way it's going to change." God said, "I want you to contest Me, and ask why?'

Peter, the Master Teacher's Pet

The earthly ministry of Jesus began with Him teaching, training, developing, and mentoring twelve men. The Bible refers to them as disciples. The word disciple comes from the Greek word *mathetes*, which means "a learner or student."

It was the tradition of Jesus' day that disciples not only learned from the teacher's lectures and discourses, but also by observing and experiencing every aspect of the teacher's very life. The disciples literally lived with the teacher. They actually watched everything the teacher did. The disciples listened to everything the teacher said. They ate with Him and traveled with Him. The disciples were in close proximity with each and every personal aspect of Jesus' (the Master Teacher's) life.

The Church exists today as a result of the obedience and faithfulness of those twelve men, minus one (Judas). So it is quite evident that Jesus was an enormously good, proficient, and effective Teacher for eleven of His twelve men to go on and change the entire world and course of all mankind. No other teacher, school, or university can claim such success and effectiveness.

However, out of the twelve men, one stood out above all the rest. It was Peter. He later became known as the apostle Peter, the one Jesus called a rock. A very unique and passionate quality about this disciple distinguished him from the other eleven. That quality was Peter's dogged determination to understand issues. He was known for always asking, why?

No doubt, the other disciples thought Peter was a big-mouth. They probably said he talked too much. They probably felt that Peter thought he was a know-it-all, but it was Peter's tendency to always ask why that caused Jesus, the Teacher, to notice this loudmouthed man and reward him with the much desired position of Teacher's pet. Notice, I said reward and not appoint.

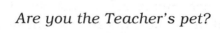

Are you the Teacher's pet?

You may be appointed to be a disciple but you have to earn the right—through diligence to know truth—to be the Teacher's pet. That's why Jesus chose Peter. Jesus knew that if enough of Peter's whys were answered, then the loudmouthed, nosey, obnoxious fisherman would eventually become a great leader and apostle that God could use to get the world's attention.

God is no respecter of persons. He does not grant favor or special privileges based on human ability or earthly accomplishments. God does show favor to those who hunger and thirst for righteousness. God favors those who thirst to know the truth and desire, no matter how great the cost, to do the will of God. It is evident that Jesus gave more attention to the development of three of the disciples—Peter, James, and John. But there was something extra significant about the relationship between Jesus and Peter, and that's what was so significant, the fact that they had a relationship.

Through Peter's persistence in asking questions, he initiated an exchange that developed a relationship between student and teacher. It caused the Teacher to spend special time with the student. Every time something sacred and significant happened in Jesus' life and ministry, Peter was there. When Moses and Elijah appeared on the Mount of Transfiguration, who was there? When Jesus raised the little girl from the dead, He put everybody, including the family, out of the room, except for three of His disciples. Who was one of those disciples? Yes, you guessed it, Peter! Everywhere and every time something exciting was going on in Jesus' life and ministry, Simon Peter was there.

Why would God spend special time with one student or child of God in comparison to any other child of God? Isn't that showing partiality? Does not God love all His children just the same? The answer to that question is yes, God does love all His children with the same degree of love. But God is a wise businessman as well as the sovereign Lord. He spends extra time, not based upon His loving one more than any other, but because the Father God knows, as well as Jesus, that you invest more time in individuals who exhibit a greater desire to know the truth, operate in those truths, and wish to influence and persuade others with that truth.

God desires for us to know His will more than we even want to know it. If we are willing to ask God why and let Him transform us into receiving His will, God will show us His favor and answer the whys of our heart.

> *God will answer the whys of our heart.*

Thoughts and Reflections

_____

_____

_____

_____

_____

_____

_____

_____

_____

_____

_____

_____

_____

_____

_____

_____

_____

_____

_____

_____

_____

_____

_____

_____
_____
_____
_____
_____
_____
_____
_____
_____
_____
_____
_____
_____
_____
_____
_____
_____
_____
_____
_____
_____
_____

Chapter 4
Purpose—The Method to the Madness

Purpose—The Method to the Madness

A *nd we know that all things work together for good to them that love God, to them who are the called according to His purpose* (Romans 8:28).

When we look at the course of our lives, it sometimes appears to be a chaotic path. The course seems to have no certain direction. Yes, even Christians often find themselves questioning the meaning and course of their lives. The things that God does in our lives, and the incidents and situations that happen in many instances, appear to be a haphazard, erratic display of a madman who gets pleasure from seeing his subjects suffer and live in despair.

But with God, this is not the case. There is a reason to the riddle. There is an answer to the question, clarity to the confusion and calmness in the chaos. A bright new day dawns after the dark night. There is a time and a purpose to everything under the sun, a method to the madness.

Knowing God's divine purpose for your life is one of the greatest assets and enablements to help understand and make sense of the perplexities and complications that seem to overwhelm you. People who possess such knowledge possess power. Jesus displayed an assurance of knowing His purpose in His life and ministry. When people sought to kill Him for His stand and boldness in declaring the truth, He didn't get fearful and back down from what He had said. No! Jesus stood His ground. Why? He knew His purpose. His purpose was to destroy the works of the devil, not be destroyed by the works of the devil.

When you are assured of your purpose, you're not fearful of men nor external personal conflicts that attempt to hinder you. Why? Because you know with confidence that sooner or later every trial, every hindering situation, and every opposing person and thing in your life will eventually and inevitably bow and submit to God's plan and purpose for your life. It's just a matter of time and circumstance.

The man who knows his purpose and God-given vision behaves in a strategic, precise, and decisive manner for spiritual warfare. Paul told Timothy to wage a good warfare by the prophecies that went before him. When you know your purpose, you won't sit and passively allow things to occur in your life that are contrary to God's purpose and vision for your life. Neither will you be so quick to get discouraged when situations bring conflict and disorder to your life. You know all things are working together for your good, because you love the Lord and are called according to His purpose. You don't become frustrated or overwhelmed by those things you can't pray away, rebuke away, cast away, fast away, confess away, or speak away. Why? Because you know that if it's in your life, God has allowed it and He wants to use it (since it's there) to transform you into the express image of Christ. He will bring you into that purpose for which you were created. All things, not some, work together for the good of those who love the Lord.

> **All** *things work together for the good of those who love God.*

Therefore, if you are confused, ready to give up, wondering what's going on and what all the turmoil and chaos you're experiencing is about, ask God, why? He just might say, "It's purpose." Maybe He's building a foundation of character in your life. Perhaps it will enable you to obtain the success and blessing that is to be poured into your life. Maybe it is a prelude to the anointing that is about to come upon you. He's got to teach you how to trust Him now, while you are in the desert, so that when you get into the promised land and people start acting funny toward you because they're jealous of the anointing on your life, you won't be afraid to cut the ungodly tie. You know your help comes not from man, but from the Lord. Do you understand what I'm saying? I know you do. If you don't, you'd better ask somebody!

But don't just ask anybody, ask the Lord! Call on the Lord and He will answer you. Go ahead. Don't be afraid. Ask Him, "Lord, why?"

Why is there so much strain, why so much struggle, so much conflict, why so much hell? Could it be because I am a man or woman of destiny? Could it be because there's a purpose, a reason for my life? Am I going through so much because I was not brought into this earth haphazardly, but there is actually some divine, ordained logic to my being? Is it true that I'm not some mistake my mother and father made one night in the heat of passion or uncontrollable lust? (If you were born out of wedlock or even as a result of rape, you're not an illegitimate child. What your parents did was illegitimate, not you. You need to know that).

"God, is it possible that You have a divine motive, a divine reason for my conception? Am I destined, purposed, called to do something great in life? Is it something that nobody else has done, something that nobody else can do but me? My brother can't do it, my sister can't do it, my husband can't do it, my wife can't do it, my pastor can't do it. Is it something so unique to my personality, so common to my life experiences, so relative to my sphere of influence, so dependent upon my color and culture, so necessary to my needs and failures and shortcomings that nobody, no one, can do it exactly the way You want it done but me?" God's response is, "You're absolutely right!" Just remember, "to whom much is given, much is required" (Luke 12:48). So get ready for the fire!

Declaring the End From the Beginning

Remember this—fix it in your mind and take it to heart: "Remember the former things, those of long ago; I am God and there is none other; I am God and there is none like me. I make known the end from the beginning, from ancient times, what is still to come. I say: My purpose will stand, and I will do all that I please" (Isaiah 46:9,10 NIV).

Wait a minute, God said He is declaring the end from the beginning. That's backward. That's out of sequence. That's out of order. You never declare the end from the beginning. Anybody who tells a good joke will tell you not to tell the punch line before the introduction. God says, "I'll do it backward for you. I declare the end from the beginning. I don't start at the foundation. I reverse the order. I start with the end of it, then I go back and start working on the beginning and make the beginning work into the end." God says, "I establish purpose and then I build procedure."

God says, "I put the victory in the heavenlies, then I start from the earth and move upward. I make sure everything is set according to My design, then I work it out according to My purpose and My plan, My will and My way." That's why God is not nervous when you are nervous, because He has set your end from the beginning. While you're struggling, groping and growling, trying to get it together, and wondering whether you will make it, God knows you're going to make it, because He has already set your end!

He has set your end from
the beginning.

A friend of mine once told me how movies are made. I thought the directors shot the movie scenes in numerical sequence, beginning with the first scene and ending with the last. That is not how it is done. Most times they will shoot the final scene of the movie first. They shoot the last scene first, then roll back the film and start shooting from the beginning, making the beginning work its way into the ending.

Built for a Habitation for God

Now therefore ye are no more strangers and foreigners, but fellow citizens with the saints, and of the household of God; And are built upon the foundation of the apostles and the prophets, Jesus Christ himself being the chief corner stone; In whom all the body fitly joined together groweth unto an holy temple in the Lord: In whom ye also are builded together for a habitation of God through the Spirit (Ephesians 2:19-22).

God's approach to destiny is first establishing the purpose, then reverting to the beginning to develop you and instruct you on how to fulfill the purpose. God works out purpose the way you would design and construct a house. If you wanted to build a massive house, you must first hire an architect. The architect takes the vision you have for the house and transforms it on paper (blueprint), establishing what it shall be before it is ever built. Then the carpenter comes in and makes the vision a reality by constructing in material form (manifesting in the present) the design (vision) that the architect has established on paper (the blueprint). Whenever the builder is confused, he refers back to the blueprint. By looking at the blueprint, he knows whether to order steel beams or wood beams, carpet or tile, brick or stucco. Whenever he is unclear about any detail or specification, all he needs to do is check the specifications and look back at what the architect has declared in the design.

I want you to know that God is the Master Architect (designer) and Master Builder all in one. He never gets confused about what is planned or how it is to be built. When God builds something, He builds it for maximum efficiency and optimal performance. We get confused and doubt the outcome. Discouraged, we often find ourselves asking God, "Why did You make me wait while other people go forth? Why does it take so long for my breakthrough to come?" God responds, "What does the blueprint say? What do the specifications call for?"

Many times we wonder why we go through so much persecution. Why do we experience so much rejection that we often feel alienated by those around us just because we love God and want to do His will? God says, "I'm building a solid foundation so you'll be able to stand under pressure and be able to go through the storms of life without being moved or shaken." God's response is simple. Anything that is made well is made slowly. "The quality must go in before the name goes on." Anything that is worth having is worth fighting for and worth working hard for.

We also have to know that God is not just building any kind of house. God is building a house of glory, a house filled with His Spirit, governed by His Word (will), and submitted to the Lordship of His Son, Jesus Christ. As tenants of that house, we are called to represent the Builder and Lord of that house by manifesting His glory on the earth. God says, "When I get through with you, when I get through nailing on you, when I get through hooking your two-by-fours together and putting windows in, when I get through hanging siding on you and placing bricks on your frame, then you are going to be a glorious edifice, a sight for the world to see." Still the house is not for us to be glorified, but that God might be exalted and glorified. "But we have this treasure in earthen vessels, that the excellency of the power may be of God, and not of us" (2 Corinthians 4:7).

Vision (Revelation) and Purpose

Where there is no revelation [vision], the people cast off restraint [perish]; but blessed is he who keeps the law [Word of God] (Proverbs 29:18).

Solomon declared in the book of Proverbs that where there is no vision (no divine and fresh revelation from God), the people perish (they lose control and cast off restraint).

If you are a person without direction, purpose, meaning, or understanding of God's specific intent for your life, it could very well mean that you lack vision. You may lack a personal revelation, which is God's divine insight into the reason for your being and the reason for your living. Vision not only gives meaning and understanding of

81

one's purpose in life, it also gives one wisdom on how to bring it to pass. Vision gives
understanding and reveals meaning to the
trials you may experience at any given time.

> *Vision gives understanding and
> reveals meaning to your trials.*

God imparts to you a revelation of His
plans for your life. That is how vision begins.
Then in some cases, God confirms that word
He spoke personally to you through a prophecy
given to you by another man or woman of
God. If you try to figure out the fulfillment of
the prophecy by looking at your present situation, circumstance or condition, it may be
hard to believe without the assurance of faith
and the witness of the Holy Spirit. Why would
it be so hard to believe? Because when God
gives you a vision, it is always too great and
complex for you in your own power and ability
to bring about. "Not by might, nor by power, but
by my Spirit saith the Lord..." (Zechariah 4:6).

God calls those things that are not as
though they were. He calls you in the present what you're going to be in the future,

and then makes you prove His Word to be true. Hence the Scripture says, "Let God be true and every man a liar" (Romans 3:4). It means you embrace what God has said about you over what everybody else has said about you, good or bad. When all has been said and done, God proves what He has said about you. It comes through His written Word and His personal revelation to you. His Word is right and everyone who speaks contrary to that word is a liar. Your life will witness the validity of God's Word if you continue to walk by faith and obey the Father. You will prove to this world that God is real and that He's able. There is nothing else in life that pleases God the Father more.

Jesus proved the validity of God's Word when He rose from the dead. This was true regardless of the Romans, Jews, skeptics, and doomsayers who did not believe in His divinity.

My brothers and sisters, you must continue to obey and serve God. You are going to show your critics and the unbelievers that you, as the servant of God, will win in the end. Some critics will bet against you and they will speak against you. They will say, "That girl ain't never gonna be nothing. Her mama was nothing. Her aunt was nothing. I knew her grandmother and she was nothing. Her granddaddy was nothing. Her father was nothing and she is going to be nothing." According to the Word of God, "If any man be in Christ, he is a new creature; old things have passed away and all things have become new" (2 Corinthians 5:17). God said that we are going to make a liar out of all of them. He says, "I will remain true (proof) and every man a liar."

Some of you have been lying to yourself, telling yourself you aren't anything. You are telling yourself you're no good, but you ought to believe God. Believe Him in spite of your feelings or emotions. Stop believing those lying prophecies of the past: relatives and friends who claimed you would never amount to anything. Stop believing people and teachers who called you stupid. Turn a deaf ear to racism which said because you're black you are not important, sexists who said because you're a woman you're not important. Stop believing the lies of men. Become renewed to the truth of God. You might have had a bad childhood and have been abused, misused, rejected, and neglected. God says forget those things that are behind you and reach forth to those things that are before you. Press towards the mark of your high calling in Christ Jesus (see Philippians 3:13-14).

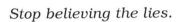

> *Stop believing the lies.*

He is our father in the sight of God in whom he believed the God that gives life to the dead and calls things that are not as though they were (Romans 4:16a,17 NIV).

No longer will you be called Abram, your name will be Abraham, for I have made you a father of many nations (Genesis 17:5 NIV).

"Calling those things that be not as though they were." The emphasis in this particular context (Romans 4:18) is not on Abraham or any believer calling things that be not as though they were, but on *God* calling those things that be not as though they were. It is God, through His Word, speaking into existence His will, not man's will. We should be very glad that it is God and not man. I wouldn't want a man to have the power to determine my future and destiny.

It is God who calls those things that be not as though they were. Our responsibility is to line our will up with His will. When we do, our lives become empowered by the grace and Spirit of God to accomplish what normally would be humanly impossible. That is the essence of authentic prophecy that comes from the heart of God.

If we continue to walk by faith, believing in the prophetic word that God has spoken over our lives, things that may seem impossible to realize in the natural shall come to pass.

The just shall live by faith, and anything that is not of faith is sin. For we walk by faith and not by sight (the physical senses, i.e. emotions, mental reasoning, or the things that we can visibly see). When God speaks a word into our lives, as far as He is concerned, it has already been accomplished. If the purpose has already been completed, the task or assignment has already been done, it is in essence a finished work. He calls those "things that be not as though they were."

Hebrews 10:14 declares that God offered Christ as the ultimate sacrifice for man's sin and has "perfected forever them that are sanctified." The word *"perfected"* in this particular passage of Scripture means in the Greek, "to bring to an end by completing or perfecting the accomplishment of bringing to completeness." This simply means that the end is already finished. It came by the supernatural power and grace given to us by what Christ accomplished during His crucifixion and resurrection.

> *Therefore we no longer have to strive in the flesh in order to fulfill God's purpose.*

Therefore we no longer have to strive in the flesh in order to fulfill God's purpose. The calling for our lives has already been determined in heaven. It is a complete and finished work. Your purpose in the sight of God is already an accomplished thing, waiting for your fulfillment. "Perfected" means completely over, settled, done, and concluded. God says, "I have perfected your life and purpose for life. I fix them, I set their course in stone. You don't have to run and see what the end is going to be." God said that it's already accomplished. The thing you're worried about performing, God said it is already done.

What about all the debris in your life? What about all of those loose ends and uncertain things that Charles Dickens talked about? He said, "Life is a tale told by a fool," but God tells a different story. He says, "All of those foolish things are going to work together for the good of them who love the Lord, to them who are the called according to His purpose" (Romans 8:28). In order to walk with God, you've got to be willing to hear some things that sound foolish. Often times, obeying God does seem like "a tale told by a fool."

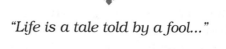

"Life is a tale told by a fool..."

God called Moses upon Mount Sinai and said, "Come on up here. I'm going to show you My purpose, what My plan shall be." Moses walked upon the mountain saying, "Yes Lord, what's going on?" The Lord said, "This is what is about to take place. There's a boy down there in your church (camp) named Aaron. Aaron is to be appointed as a high priest. I'm making him an outfit: a garment symbolizing my pattern of holiness, righteousness, and My set and divine way of communicating to My people. The outfit will have a breastplate with twelve stones, each one representing one of the twelve tribes of Israel—My chosen people. I'm getting him together, girding his loins about with truth. When I get through with him, he shall be a glorious and beautiful sight for eyes to see. Aaron shall be the one who will be able to go in and out before Me." Anybody can attempt to come in before God, but it takes a holy person to come out living. God told Moses when nobody else can be in His presence and live, Aaron will be anointed to come in and go out alive.

Aaron sounds like a pretty good fellow, but while God was declaring to Moses about Aaron's perfected state, He was already taking care of Aaron's end, calling those things that are not as though they were. Aaron was down at the bottom of the mountain, working on the beginning. If you were to judge from Aaron's beginning, you would not believe what was promised to this guy. As a matter of fact, the guy was down the mountain engrossed in idol worship, worshiping a golden calf. The guy just didn't have it going on. He was an idolater. He was the head of the hypocrites, president of the failures, chairman of the defeated, busy building a golden calf unto a strange god.

When Moses came down the mountain, he began to build up Aaron, exhorting him on who he was and what God called him to do and be. Moses got the revelation of the end. Moses says, "Hey man, (I'm paraphrasing), oohhh God has designed an outfit for you.... Blood, you're going to be laid out, you are going to be too sharp."

I know what you probably would have said. Something like, "Lord God, do You know where he is? Do You know what he's doing?" You don't believe God knew what he was doing? Remember God sets the end from the beginning, calling those things that are not as though they were. God declares even to you today, as you read this book, that, "In spite of what you've done, in spite of how you've failed, in spite of how you've messed up, in spite of how you have suffered, in spite of how many times you have given up and almost died, I want you to know that My grace is sufficient for you. My grace will enable you to be victorious and make it through to complete your journey (purpose).

I've shed blood for you and given sacrifices for you. When I get through washing, molding, and making you into what I've already declared you are, you will show the world how glorious I am."

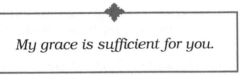

My grace is sufficient for you.

That No Flesh Shall Glory in His Sight

Brothers, think of what you were when you were called. Not many of you were wise by human standards; not many were influential; not many were of noble birth. But God chose the foolish things of the world to shame the wise; God chose the weak things of the world to shame the strong. He chose the lowly things of this world and the despised things and the things that are not—to nullify the things that are.... That no flesh should glory in His presence (1 Corinthians 1:26-28 NIV; 1:29 KJV).

God doesn't seek to manifest His glory and glorious works through those whom the world perceives as great and wonderful. He boldly declares without apology or apprehension that "My ways are not your ways, my thoughts are higher than your thoughts" (see Isaiah 55:8). When people seek individuals to do great and monumental things, they look for those who have great education, wealth, prestige, and honor; a man of great nobility. But God selects those who are like bums. He chooses those whom the world has rejected; those who have been ostracized and alienated from family, friends, and peers; those who are constantly criticized. God takes them and makes them and infuses them with His power, revelation, and wisdom so that they can be wondrously educated in the things of God. This occurs so that they can greatly change and affect the things of the world.

God considers those of no account, those nobody expects to be anything; those whose family, friends, and relatives have thrown away and given up on. God takes those who are fearful and don't believe in themselves and makes them men and women of greatness with wealth, prestige, and honor— mighty men and women of valor! These are men and women like Abraham, Joseph, Gideon, Jacob, Peter, Deborah, Ruth, Esther, Mary, William J. Seymour, Oral Roberts, Bishop Mason of the Church of God in Christ, Aimee Semple McPherson of the Foursquare Church, and Kathryn Kuhlman, just to name a few. Why does God do this? Why does God use the rejected and the despised?

It's a simple but profound answer: that He, God, would get all the glory and not man, "that no flesh should glory in his presence." For the Word of God says that "we have this treasure in earthen vessels, that the excellency of the power may be of God and not of us" (2 Corinthians 4:7). It is God and not you. God says, "When I bring you out, your critics will know it was Me. I'm going to wait until you fail; I'm going to wait until you lose confidence in yourself, your education, your job, your influential title, your résumés, your friends, your family, your doctrines, your creed, and your denominational affiliation. When you've lost hope in everything earthly and feel totally worthless and are in complete despair, then I'm going to stretch forth My right hand. I'm going to pick your feet up out of the miry clay. I'm going to place you on a rock to stay. When nobody else will praise Me, praise will continually be in your mouth, because you are going to know it was My right hand, and My holy arm that brought you victory. It was I who brought you out. It was I who gave you a breakthrough, and not yourself nor the help of man."

Give God the glory.

Do you still wonder why you have had to go through all the pain and hell you have been experiencing since getting serious with God and vowing to obey Him, no matter what the cost? The reason is that you would no longer place confidence in the flesh, for it is God who works in you both to will and to do His good will and pleasure. But in all things we must give Him the praise, not man, "that no flesh should glory in His presence" (1 Corinthians 1:29).

Thoughts and Reflections

_____

_____

_____

_____

_____

_____

_____

_____

_____

_____

_____

_____

_____

_____

_____

_____

_____

_____

_____

_____

_____

_____

_____

_____

_____

_____

_____

_____

_____

_____

_____

_____

_____

_____

_____

_____

_____

_____

_____

_____

_____

_____

_____

_____

_____

_____

_____
_____
_____
_____
_____
_____
_____
_____
_____
_____
_____
_____
_____
_____
_____
_____
_____
_____
_____
_____
_____
_____
_____
_____

Chapter 5
Because You Are Anointed

Because You Are Anointed

Why do the heathen rage, and the people imagine a vain thing? The kings of the earth set themselves, and the rulers take counsel together, against the Lord, and against his anointed, saying, let us break their bands asunder, and cast away their cords from us. He that sitteth in the heavens shall laugh: the Lord shall have them in derision. Then shall he speak unto them in his wrath, and vex them in his sore displeasure. Yet have I set my king upon my holy *hill of Zion. I will declare the decree: the Lord hath said unto me, Thou art my Son; this day have I begotten thee. Ask of me, and I shall give thee the heathen for thine inheritance, and the uttermost parts of the earth for thy possession* (Psalm 2:1-8).

Why do the heathen rage and the people imagine a vain thing? The actual question in this text is not King David asking God the motivation of those who take counsel (conspire) to come against the Lord and His anointed. More importantly, it is David asking God why He allows it to happen. "God, why do You allow the heathen to rage, and why do You let the rulers and kings of the earth set themselves against You and against Your anointed? Why God, why?"

The Question Is Why?

Why does God allow His anointed to suffer so greatly? After all, the sole motivation of the anointed is to do the will of God. You would think that if the primary desire in the life of the anointed is to please their heavenly

Father, the least He could do is protect and preserve them. You would think God would stop the persecution, mistreatment, and abuse of the heathens and phony church folks. But the truth of the matter is that God allows, and in most cases sends, His anointed through more than all others. An intelligent question is, "God, why?'

The anointed might say, "Why do You let this mess happen when I'm obeying you? Why do You let people treat me like this? God, what's up with that? Are You a sadist who enjoys inflicting pain on others? Oh God, why allow these heathens to trip on me like this? I mean, after all, I'm a man of God, I'm a woman of God. I don't have to take this kind of treatment from some stupid unsaved employer who doesn't even respect the fact that I'm called, appointed, and anointed. Hey, these people don't even know You. I do.

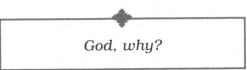

God, why?

Therefore, I should be afforded special privileges. I should not have to wait until I mature and develop character to get whatsoever I desire—I'm a king's kid! I should be able to just name it and claim it. I have the keys to the kingdom. I can call what I want into existence. I thought all I had to do is say the Word, right?" But you know what God's response is to all that selfishness and flesh? **No...I...don't...think...so!"**

Let us look at the psalmist's question in this passage and address each point, one by one.

"Whys" of the Anointed

The kings of the earth set themselves, and the rulers take counsel together [conspiring together], against the Lord, and against his anointed (Psalm 2:2).

"Against the Lord" The most prevailing sin of all mankind is the sin of selfishness...the idolizing of self (self idolatry). Selfishness is the epitome of satanic, demonic, and rebellious sinful motivations and behavior. Observing the power and majesty of Almighty God, satan became jealous of the Lord's glory. Satan sought to instigate a mutiny in heaven.

Jealousy is the manifestation of insecurity and dissatisfaction with ones calling and self-worth. When you don't know your purpose, you become discontent and many times become envious of another's success. Jealousy and bitter envying are the root cause of the spirit of competition. That spirit presently plagues many in church leadership and those aspiring to positions of leadership. Everybody wants to be number one, the top dog, the head honcho, the man or woman in demand.

So in our desire to be number one, we covet, lust, and compete for another's position, status, or possessions. Why do we do this? Because we want everybody to look at us, to like us, to admire us, to respect us, to worship us. Before we know it, we've become drunk with selfish ambition and, like satan, our hidden motives of the heart become the attitude of rebellion against who and what God has called us to be and do. If we don't come to our senses and repent, we will inevitably become deceived and overwhelmed with the lust for power, prestige, position, and possessions. We no longer aspire to love the Lord with all our heart, soul, strength, and mind. The confession and attitude of our heart reflect the sentiment of satan: "I will exalt myself above the throne of God, above the throne of my husband, above the throne of my employer or supervisor. My church will be bigger than the Baptist church down the street. I'm going to be more popular and bigger than the other TV evangelist. I will... I, I, I, I will exalt myself."

Because you were not patient enough to wait on God's timing (even though you've been called, you need to wait until you are sent), you've aligned yourself with the wicked rulers of the day and taken counsel against the Lord. Why? Selfishness!

"And against His anointed." It is without exception, absolutely necessary for the anointed to suffer. The moment you begin to accept and understand this, you will begin to rejoice in tribulation. I know this doesn't sit well with much of what we've been taught in reference to our victory in Christ. We do have victory in Christ, but we must understand that there has to be a battle fought in order to gain a victory. There is no victory without war. Also you have to know that just as God has promised to supply all our needs according to His riches in glory, He also has promised us trials and tribulations in this life. Tribulations and trials serve, by the aid of the Holy Spirit, a divine purpose. The purpose is death. Death? That's right, I mean death—death to the flesh.

If you are going to walk in the anointing and presence of God, you must be dead to self. In order to be alive to Christ, you must first yield to the sanctifying work of the Holy Spirit and die to the works of the flesh. Why? So that no flesh may glory in His sight. Before a man or woman is dead to self, they are occupied and consumed with self and how they can please themselves. They make a conscious decision to walk in their own understanding, instead of acknowledging the Lord and being directed by His wisdom.

Submission + Suffering + Obedience + Praise = Anointing

And Samuel said, "Hath the Lord a great delight in burnt offerings and sacrifices, as in obeying the voice of the Lord? Behold, to obey is better than sacrifice, and to harken than the fat of rams. For rebellion is as the sin of witchcraft, and stubbornness is as iniquity and idolatry. Because thou hast rejected the word of the Lord, he has also rejected thee from being King (1 Samuel 15:22-23).

Like King Saul, selfish Christians are charismatic witches. They rebel against totally submitting to the Lordship of Christ Jesus (the Anointed). Like King Saul, selfish, carnal Christians and Christian leaders are idolaters of self. They stubbornly insist upon doing things their way instead of God's way. Selfish people (self-idolaters) sometimes are a god unto themselves. Just like King Saul and Samson the judge, they will awake one day to find that the glory (the Anointing) has departed (that is, if they were ever anointed in the first place).

Anointed people are in great demand by those who need the touch of God in their life. Because anointed people have the ability to draw from the resources of God's miracle-working power in time of desperate need, people have a tendency to worship and make idols out of them. But God says He shares His glory with no one. God is a jealous God. God will not bestow His Holy Spirit upon some flaky, selfish Christian who is engrossed with selfish ambition, trying to build a kingdom at the expense of using God's anointing. Many ministries try to build their own personal kingdom, while rationalizing that they are building God's Church. The devil is a liar and the truth is not in him.

---

*Anointed people are
in great demand.*

Why are the anointed persecuted? Anointed people are free people. The Word of God says where the Spirit of the Lord is there is liberty (see 2 Corinthians 3:17). Wicked leadership and stubborn, sedate people, who have taken counsel against the Lord, do not like free people, because free people can't be controlled.

Anointed people are full of the Holy Ghost. Life in the Holy Ghost is righteousness, peace, and joy. Anointed people are people who have been burdened by the cross of Calvary and are no longer bound by the sins and embarrassments of old lifestyles.

Anointed men and women of God know that because of the precious blood shed by Jesus Christ; they have right-standing with the Father. When they think about the goodness of Jesus, and all that He's done for them, their very soul cries out, "Hallelujah!" They begin to praise God with unrestrained zeal and passion. That, my brothers and sisters, is what gives you joy unspeakable and full of glory, the anointed presence of the Holy Spirit.

Controlling people (like those rulers who wanted to keep the people from praising Jesus) find that type of ecstatic praise to be very irritating and irrational. They want you to be composed and dignified at all times. Why? Because instead of giving praise and worship to Jesus, they unknowingly (and some knowingly) want you to praise them—the great "Doctor So-and-So" and the wonderful "Mother Who-dun-it." But again, the devil is a liar!

The heathen declare "Let us break their bands asunder, and cast away their cords from us" (Psalm 2:3). The word bands means chains and cords or fetters attached around the feet to restrict movement. The psalmist signifies unity in the illustration. The anointed people of God often find themselves in conflict with those who have personal agendas that are contrary to the will of God.

Persecution is a mandatory by-product of being anointed of God. You would think that since your motivations and intentions are only to do God's will and minister to God's people, everybody, especially Christian folks, would love you and appreciate you so much. Not so. The all-encompassing question comes to mind, Why not?

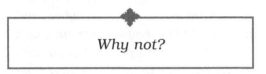

Why not?

The anointing of God has the innate and wonderful ability to soften hard hearts, break stiff necks, crush pride, and tear down the walls of strife and division. This inevitably will bring sincere men and women to repentance. A repented heart is soft and gentle. Gentle hearts are receptive to reconciliation. Reconciliation is the hallmark of love. Love and forgiveness are the cornerstone and foundation that build. So why do the heathen seek to divide the people of God? Simply put, so there will not be any anointing. Nothing can wither up and dry out the fresh spring well of the Spirit's anointing faster than strife, division (two different visions), and discord. The Bible says, "Six things does the Lord hate and the seventh is an abomination," the seventh thing being those who sow discord among the brethren (the saints of God). But when we get in accord, seeking the will of God, He will always, almost without exception, manifest Himself.

> *And when the day of Pentecost was fully come, they were all with one accord in one place. And suddenly there came a sound from heaven as of a rushing mighty wind, and it filled all the house where they were sitting. And there appeared unto them cloven tongues like as of fire, and it sat upon each of them. And they were all filled with the Holy Ghost, and began to speak with other tongues, as the Spirit gave them utterance (Acts 2:1-4).*

Unity evolves around truth-seeking believers who are committed to knowing the heart of Christ. Unity brings about the Spirit's power and anointing.

He That Sitteth in the Heavens Laughs

God is pleased and obsessed with being glorified and receiving glory from His creation. Many children of God have become overwhelmed with bewilderment and are confused as to why bad things always seem to happen to good people. But the answer is simple, my friend. God wants to be glorified. So every now and then you may find yourself tempted and pursued like a fugitive, wanted by the devil. The pressure, stress, and strain in your life may make you feel like a hunk of cheese on a mouse trap, ready to be eaten by the enemy. You may get the idea that God is using you like a pawn on a chess board, which is a game called life that you have no control over and cannot win.

The devil gets happy because he thinks you're down for the count. But, God laughs! Why? Because God already knows that He will not allow you to go through anything, or be subjected to anything, beyond your anointing. (See 1 Corinthians 10:13). God gives you ability to bear it. That's why He laughs and lets the devil sometimes have at you. God knows you're faithful. God knows that it's just a matter of time before satan pushes you so far that you will fall right back into the lap of goodness and mercy.

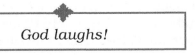

God laughs!

Why goodness and mercy? Because goodness and mercy are praise partners. They testify and witness to the goodness of God. They remind us of the fact that no matter how hard the battle, how difficult the trial, we can have assurance that God the Father will never leave us. He will never forsake us. Goodness makes us confident to know that if we will only be still and wait on God, we will eventually and inevitably see the salvation of the Lord. Goodness is God's guarantee that we will get that massive, needed, and overdue "breakthrough."

What about mercy? Sometimes because of being weary from the battle, overwhelmed by the cares of life, or simply just because of disobedience or dead works of our flesh, we occasionally give in to temptations. We yield to the lust of the flesh. We might as well be truthful about it. Even though we are not just "sinners saved by grace," we do miss the mark every now and then. In truth, we are the righteousness of God in Christ Jesus and we have right standing with the Father. However, sometimes we miss it by sinning in our flesh, not our spirit. It is in those times that mercy steps in through the person and blood of Jesus Christ. Mercy pleads our case before the Father. The Bible says we have an advocate with the Father, that "if we confess our sins, he is faithful and just to forgive us of our sins and cleanse us from all unrighteousness" (1 John 1:9). Scripture also says, "There is therefore now no condemnation to them which are in Christ Jesus, who walk not after the flesh, but after the Spirit" (Romans 8:1).

Mercy steps in
through Jesus Christ.

Mercy says, "God, I know he was disobedient; I know he didn't do what You told him to, but can You find it in Your heart to show him just a little mercy? After all, Daddy, he is Your child and You know he really loves You. To the best of his human frailty, he does try to obey You and serve You, so if You would (and I know because of Your goodness You can), will You please forgive him and show him Your mercy? Not just some mercy, or any mercy, but Your mercy."

God's mercy is not like any kind of mercy. You cannot possibly compare God's mercy with man's mercy because God's mercy is not based on the condition of what we've done. It is based on what God has done through the shed blood of Jesus Christ. It is through the blood of Jesus Christ that we have redemption of our sins. Our goody-two-shoes behavior doesn't count. So now, we're truly liberated because we no longer have to worry about being good enough. We are accepted and beloved of the Father. Now that's something to shout about!

Man's mercy is a different case. Man's mercy is based upon your ability to redeem yourself and change your wicked ways. God's mercy and forgiveness are based on His will to redeem you and His ability to empower you with His Spirit to transform you from your wicked ways. Man is inconsistent. God is consistent. Man is wishy-washy. God is stable. Man is flaky and most of the time, helpless. God is wonderful and all of the time able.

David told the Lord, "When I sin, please let me fall into Your hands and not the hands of man. For man is wicked, cruel and without mercy, but God is loving and forgiving, showing mercy to those who call on His name" (see 2 Samuel 24:14).

God knows that if He can get you in enough trouble with the devil; enough need and lack in your finances; under just the right amount of pressure; experience just so much pain; and go through enough stress and strain, He knows you'll cry out for help. "The Lord's hand is not shortened, that it cannot save; neither his ear heavy, that it cannot hear" (Isaiah 59:1). God wants to build in you faithfulness. Your heavenly Father knows that if He can just get you to the end of yourself, you will eventually begin to stop leaning on the arm of your flesh. You will begin to honestly trust in Him with all your heart, and lean not on your own understanding. But you will in all your ways truly begin to acknowledge Him, not only as Savior, but as Lord (Proverbs 3:5,6).

The Church as a whole must understand it is absolutely imperative we accept the truth of God's ultimate and universal purpose for all who call on the name of Jesus. We are to be conformed and transformed into the express image of Christ even as Christ was the express image of the Father (see Hebrews 1:3). Hebrews says that Jesus was and is the express image of God. That means that Christ represented the perfect and complete person and mind of God the Father.

> *Be conformed and transformed into the express image of Christ...*

Our ultimate purpose, as citizens of the kingdom of God and ambassadors of Christ, is to be perfect and complete expressions of the person and power of Jesus Christ. We are to manifest God's will on earth as it is in heaven. It is way past the hour that we accept this reality. The mandate of the kingdom is the ministry of reconciliation—reconciling man back to God. We must first die to the image of ourselves in order to be transformed into the image of Christ. This is one of many, if not the primary reason, that God allows us to go through trials and temptations by the enemy. I said He *allows* you to be tempted of the devil; I didn't say He initiates the tempting. If you're not tempted by evil, how do you know you can resist evil? Also, if you're not being tempted by the enemy, it could very well mean that you've submitted to the enemy. Temptation, in and of itself, is not sin. It's surrendering to temptation that is sin.

When we truly represent God, we express His will and manifest His glory. This is why God laughs at the futile attempts of satan to come against and destroy His children. The devil becomes excited when we're at the point of giving up and giving in, ready to throw in the towel. When we're desperate, the devil really believes we will stop trying to live right, stop praying, stop trying to be a Christian, and backslide.

But God Laughs

Why? God knows that when we've come to the end of our rope, when we've reached our weakest point and become desperate, it is only then that we totally, unequivocally, without question or complaint, absolutely rely on and trust in Him. Trust Him when you've prayed every prayer you know how. Trust Him when you've quoted every Scripture you've ever memorized. Trust Him when you've made every faith-filled confession you can muster. Trust Him when you've done all that you know to do and the situation still hasn't changed or there seems to be no healing, salvation, or deliverance in sight. God tells you the same thing He said to the great apostle Paul, "Don't worry, be happy. For when you've done all that you know to do, just stand." "My grace is sufficient for thee: for my strength is made perfect in weakness" (2 Corinthians 12:9a).

Trust Him.

Therefore, let us, as anointed men and women of God, take the attitude of Paul, "Most gladly therefore will I rather glory in my infirmities, that the power of Christ may rest upon me. Therefore I take pleasure in infirmities, in reproaches, in necessities, in persecutions, in distresses for Christ's sake: for when I am weak, then am I strong" (2 Corinthians 12:9b, 10).

So why do I rejoice in tribulations, trials, and afflictions? Because when I get weak, that's when I get anointed!

Thoughts and Reflections

_____

_____

_____

_____

_____

_____

_____

_____

_____

_____

_____

_____

_____

_____

_____

_____

_____

_____

_____

_____

_____

_____

_____
_____
_____
_____
_____
_____
_____
_____
_____
_____
_____
_____
_____
_____
_____
_____
_____
_____
_____
_____
_____
_____
_____
_____

_____

_____

_____

_____

_____

_____

_____

_____

_____

_____

_____

_____

_____

_____

_____

_____

_____

_____

_____

_____

_____

_____

_____

_____

Chapter 6
Persist and Persevere

Persist and Persevere

Persistence—Holding Fast to Your Confession of Faith

L et us draw near with a true heart in full assurance of faith, having our hearts sprinkled from an evil conscience, and our bodies washed with pure water. Let us hold fast the profession of our faith without wavering; for he is faithful that promise (Hebrews 10:22,23).

My brothers and sisters, you may be going through hell right now. The fact of the matter is you must accept the reality that God the Father, Creator of Heaven and Earth, is trying to mold you and transform you. God wants to change you into what He has declared as His purpose for your life, and that which He spoke about in His written Word. That word is: You are more than a conqueror through Jesus Christ who loves you (see Romans 8:37). You are the righteousness of God in Christ Jesus (see Romans 3:22). Greater is He that is in you than he that is in the world (see 1 John 4:4). You have the power to tread upon serpents and scorpions and over all the power of the enemy (see Luke 10:19). No weapon formed against you shall prosper (see Isaiah 54:17). You really are the head and not the tail, above and not beneath, the rich and not the poor (see Deuteronomy 28:13).

You, my brothers and sisters, are indeed what God's Word says you are. You are to appropriate what the Word says you are and what the Word says you have. It involves more than just "believing and receiving!"

You've got to be able to persist and move forward in the will of God for your life. Your persistence must continue even when everything seems to be falling apart and when it looks like nothing is turning out right. Stop whining. Learn to stand up under pressure. Set the vision of God before you like a flint and move forward full speed ahead with the plan of God. I don't care how many times the lights get cut off. I don't care how many times the water and heat get turned off. I don't care how many times the rent is over-due. I don't care if you don't have a car and have to use the bus to get from point A to point B. I don't care if you have to eat red beans and rice three days a week just to survive. Forget the dumb stuff! If God gave you a vision for something, you've got to know the devil will not sit idly by. You have to fight the devil for the vision, tooth and toenail, every single step of the way. It's less intense to take the easy road, the road of trusting in the things and systems of this world. It's always convenient to call mommy and daddy, to get a loan, or to compromise your standards and morals for a promotion on the job. It may seem justifiable to embez-zle money from the saints of God to make your church or ministry grow. After all, you're just trying to do the work of the Lord, and they owe it to you.

Forget the dumb stuff!

Know, my brothers and sisters, that the world has a particular road to success. The way of the wicked is the path that leads to spiritual, moral, and physical destruction.

The path to true spiritual, moral, physical and economic success is the road less traveled. It's the straight and narrow road. In order to truly increase, you must first decrease. Before a seed buds and bears fruit, it must first fall into the ground and die. In order to gain your life, you must first lose it for Christ's sake. If you really want to know Christ in the power of His resurrection, you must have fellowship with His sufferings. We've got to stop being enemies of the cross. We must take up our cross and bear it daily. The going has always been rough, so we might as well set our minds to get tough. Don't just praise God when everything seems fine and well. We've got to start learning how to cry out to Him in praise even when it appears we're going through hell.

God wants to get you to the point that you become as faithful as the patriarch Job. When anointed people get under pressure, like Job they say, "Even though He slay me yet shall I praise Him" He wants you to differ from the children of Israel, who only murmured and complained when He brought them out of Egyptian bondage. God knows you're anointed, and anointed people have the qualities of Moses, Paul, Stephen, and Jesus. They are faithful, regardless of the afflictions, unto death. In this, God is greatly glorified.

Sonship Manifested Through Suffering

Matthew 3:17 says, "Thou art my son and this day have I begotten thee." I'm not saying that suffering makes one a son. I am a son of God because I have believed on and received the Lord Jesus Christ as my Savior and Lord (see John 1:12). But there is something about suffering that makes your sonship evident. There is something about suffering that will bring glory to your life. The apostle Paul said he gloried in tribulations. There is something about suffering that builds determination in your life. It is determination that says, "I don't care how you feel about me, what you think about me, or even who's looking at me. When I feel the need or urge to, I'm going to praise the Lord. You may want me to be quiet, calm and controlled, but I'm going to bless Him anyway.

I've been through too much to let somebody bind or hinder me from giving God praise. The Lord has delivered me and seen me through too many unbearable situations. I've had to shed too many tears of heartache and pain to let somebody stop me from giving God the praise and honor that is due only Him. My situation was so bad that only God could have brought me out."

Apostle Paul gloried in tribulations.

God says, "You're My child and now it's time for show-and-tell. I'm going to resurrect you. I'm going to bring you up out of your downtrodden situation. I'm going to deliver you. I'm going to bring you out. They said you would never be anything, but I'm going to raise you up." God says, "All the chaos, the unresolved issues, and the unexplained situations will begin to make sense. All of it. You had to go through this so you would suffer enough to die." After the dying process, God will say, "I'm going to bring you to a place of resurrection. It's going to be you, but it's not going to be you. You're going to have a new mind and a new attitude. You're going to be able to understand My dealings and workings. You are going to comprehend and clearly grasp My purpose for your life and ministry. You will soon have the vision to see clearly and objectively My will in your life."

God wants to bring you to the point where you will not only be strong when troubles come, but stable. He wants you to stop worrying all the time about the outcome of things. The next time something devastating happens in your life, you need not get upset. You should say, "I have been through this before. I've been lonely before, I've had to cry before, I've suffered before. I have had to press my way through before, and I found out that all things work together for good to them that love the Lord and are called according to His purpose. I'm going to stand here and wait and see how God brings me out. I don't know when the breakthrough will come, or from where it will come, but I do know it's coming. Whom God will use, I may not know.

Where the check will come from, I may not know. Through whom God will give me favor, I may not be certain. There is one

133

thing I can be assured of and that is this—if I can just wait on the Lord, He's going to bring me out victoriously. If He has to move a mountain, do a miracle, or create a wonder, I have faith and confidence that my God will do it. If I just continue to persist, be steadfast, unmovable and always abound in the work and will of the Lord, I am coming out...and I'll come out shining. He will, to His glory and honor, bring me through it, and I will continue to praise Him through it all."

Perseverance

Beloved, think it not strange concerning the fiery trial which is to try you, as though some strange thing happened to you: But rejoice, inasmuch as you are partakers of Christ's sufferings; that, when his glory shall be revealed, ye may be glad also with exceeding joy. If ye be reproached for the name of Christ, happy are ye; for the Spirit of glory and of God resteth upon you (1 Peter 4:12-14c).

David asked the question, "Why do the kings of the earth set themselves against

God's anointed?" (See Psalm 2:2.) As we have learned, it is necessary for the anointed to suffer. When you begin to understand this principle of the kingdom, it will cause you to rejoice in tribulation.

There is a root that produces an embalming agent that the Bible calls myrrh. Myrrh was one of the major ingredients used by the priests and prophets to anoint and ordain people, places, and things that were set aside for the sacred service of the Lord. Myrrh is a fragrant substance. It grows from a small stick-like shrub. On the surface, there's nothing spectacular about it. It's not appealing to look upon. It is just a rootlike shrub. Myrrh is also very bitter to taste. But if you throw it down on the ground and crush it, it exudes a lovely, wonderful, and heavenly fragrance.

The more you crush it, press on it, bruise it, and beat it, the more wonderful and delightful the smell that emanates. The more it becomes battered, bruised, and treaded upon, the more potent the release. It's nothing delightful to the eyes. It's a shattered root, but it sure smells good. God says in this hour to His servants, "If I'm going to use you to show forth My glory and My power, I'm going to have to crush you to extract My fragrance (the anointing) out of you. Trust Me in the crushing because when the crushing is all over with, it's going to bring about My purpose. I'm going to bring death so that I can bring life. I'm going to make you so aromatic that whenever you come into a room people will know that they have just encountered the presence of Almighty God."

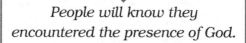

People will know they encountered the presence of God.

God wants you filled and flowing with His anointing so much that He can send you into the stinky places of this world. When you enter these places, you will bring forth life that flows from the fragrance of God's presence.

Lazarus is an example of this principle. He was dead. Lazarus' sisters said, "Lord, by now he stinketh!" Jesus took His time to see about His friend Lazarus. The sisters thought Jesus' arrival was too late. They, like us, had not yet learned how to trust God in waiting. But when the aroma of Jesus' anointing hit the grave-yard, the power of His anointing brought life where there was death. If Jesus had not specif-ically called Lazarus by name, everyone and everything would have risen. God's Word and Spirit force life into existence. God says, "I'm going to sweeten you up so when you go in the fragrance of My presence, you will fill the entire atmosphere. The place will light up because you walked in."

If you want to be anointed, you've got to be crushed. If you want to be anointed, you're going to have to go through some things. Have you been through something? If you really want to be blessed by the anointing, let somebody who has been through something preach, teach, or sing. If you are among all of those who say hallelujah just to be saying hallelujah because a man or woman of God preaches, you don't have any flavor. All of you who have been beaten, battered, shaken, crushed, rejected, and ostracized have a fragrance coming out of you sweeter than the honey in the honeycomb. It's better than the Rose of Sharon—unto God a sweet-smelling savor in His nostrils. And the more you're afflicted, the more anointed you will become.

Be Ye Steadfast

Therefore, my beloved brethren be ye steadfast, unmovable, always abounding in the work of the Lord, forasmuch as you know that your labor is not in vain in the Lord (1 Corinthians 15:58).

Thoughts and Reflections

_____

_____

_____

_____

_____

_____

_____

_____

_____

_____

_____

_____

_____

_____

_____

_____

_____

_____

_____

_____

_____

_____

_____
_____
_____
_____
_____
_____
_____
_____
_____
_____
_____
_____
_____
_____
_____
_____
_____
_____
_____
_____
_____
_____

_____
_____
_____
_____
_____
_____
_____
_____
_____
_____
_____
_____
_____
_____
_____
_____
_____
_____
_____
_____
_____
_____
_____

Chapter 7
Go Forth!

Go Forth!

*A*nd being let go, they went to their own company, and reported all that the chief priest and elders had said unto them. And when they heard that, they lifted up their voices to God with one accord, and said, Lord, thou art God, which has made heaven, and earth, and the sea, and all that is in them: who by the mouth of thy servant David hast said, Why do the heathen rage, and the people imagine vain things? The kings of the earth stood up, and the rulers *were gathered together against the Lord, and against his Christ. For of a truth against thy holy child Jesus, whom thou hast anointed, both Herod, and Pontius Pilate, with Gentiles, and the people of Israel, were gathered together, for to do whatsoever thy hand and thy counsel determined before to be done. And now Lord, behold their threatenings: and grant unto thy servants, that with all boldness they may speak thy word, By stretching forth thine hand to heal; and that signs and wonders may be done by the name of thy holy child Jesus. And when they had prayed, the place was shaken where they were assembled together; and they were all filled with the Holy Ghost, and they spoke the word of God with boldness* (Acts 4: 23-31).

Peter and John had been in jail for preaching the gospel and healing a lame man in the name of Jesus. The Bible says that God had been greatly glorified in the hearts of the people as a result of the miracle the Lord had wrought through Peter and John. The rulers of the city sought to punish the apostles for preaching in Jesus' name, but God had come

through and performed a miracle on their be-
half, granting their release.

Now you know how it is when the Church
comes under persecution. They come to fellowship service acting real funny! So Brother
Peter said to himself, "I better get a good
message for this service. Let me pull something here from the book of Psalms. I'll use
the passage when King David was all perplexed and confused, asking the Lord, 'Why
do the heathen rage?'"

Peter began to preach this message to
them about God and purpose. Peter and
John still had the prints of chains on their
wrists, had been in jail all night long, and
had probably been without food or water.
Here was a chance to really be downtrodden
and discouraged. Instead, Peter, the former
"Teacher's pet," started preaching to them
about purpose. He began (and I paraphrase):
"You know folks, we just had a wonderful experience of God's Spirit as we were partying
(celebrating) at the Pentecost festival, and as
expected, we ran into a little trouble with the
law for jamming (singing and praising) too
loud, too hard, and too strong. We experienced a trial that caused us a little bit of

pain and discomfort, but you're going to see God turn it around and make it work for your good."

The people were listening to Peter preach. Peter was excited, telling them about God's purpose. Peter continued, "Brethren, if you just pursue God's purpose, God's going to bless you with a divine destiny. God's going to show you how to come out of this. He is going to reveal to you how to be delivered." The Bible said that when they heard the Word, all of a sudden they began to believe what God had said about them. Let me say this, you've got to believe that you're coming out of your dilemma. You've got to believe that you're coming out of your trial and test with a passing and perfect score.

> *God will bless you with a divine destiny.*

Do you know what happened when Peter got through preaching about God's purpose in their lives and answering their *whats* and *whys.* The Bible said that they got together and prayed. They prayed and prayed and prayed.

They prayed until the whole house was shaken. They prayed until the floor began to shake. They prayed until the foundation began to tremble.

When you're praying for God's deliverance, you can't be praying little cute and sophisticated prayers. When you're in a desperate and urgent situation, an educational, intellectual, and dignified sounding prayer won't cut it.

When you are really in trouble, you don't have time for those superficial, cute, impressive, and intellectual-sounding types of prayers like: "Oh, thou everlasting Father, Ruler of the universe, the I AM that I AM of Israel, the Consolation, the Hope of the world, the Mighty One. I come unto your auspicious grace, through the torn veil that was rent in the temple. I lay my particulars before Your abilities, because through necessity I am able to determine Your preeminent preexistent greatness, and I lay before You the desires of mine most fragile heart, knowing that Thou are always attentive to the prayers of Thine saints. Oh, Most Merciful..." God says, "Shut up that insincere and phony mess!" When you are in real need of help, you don't have time for all that junk.

What you need is a desperate "Help, Lord! Please help now!" That nonsense may be all right for some backward preacher trying to impress a bunch of flaky religious people, but when you are in serious trouble, burdened with a serious need, you've got to pray until you go beyond the limit of your flesh. You've got to pray until your will begins to line up with His will, until your thoughts become God's thoughts and your ways become His ways.

> *I AM that I AM—the Hope of the world.*

Sometimes we're confronted with problems and situations that are so complex that they very often go beyond our ability to understand and comprehend. That's exactly why the apostle Paul said, "the Spirit also helpeth our infirmities: for we know not what we should pray for as we ought: but the Spirit itself maketh intercession for us with groanings which cannot be uttered" (Romans 8:26). By infirmities, Paul means human weakness that indicates the inability to produce the desired results or fulfill the necessary need. The notation for infirmities in the *Ryrie Study*

Bible, as it relates to Romans 8:26, says that these particular infirmities are "our inability to pray intelligently about 'certain' situations."

Regardless of how well you know the Word, and regardless of how prolific you are at praying and quoting the Word, you've got to know that there will come a time when you will not know what it is that you need in order to rectify a situation in accordance with the will of God. As the saints of God, if we are serious about submitting to and obeying the will of God for our lives, we need to have total reliance upon the Holy Spirit to direct us in all our daily affairs, "because [the Spirit] maketh intercession for the saints according to the will of God" (Romans 8:27c ASV).

They prayed and the place they were assembled in began to shake. God filled them with the Holy Ghost and they started speaking the Word with boldness. The basic adherence to the "Word of Faith" doctrine, contrary to all the doomsayers, is a true and authentic biblical principal. However, you can't just speak the Word out of your flesh and expect it to work the will of God for your life. You have got to be, without exception, led of the Spirit in all that you do in God. The Bible says that "the letter alone killeth but the Spirit giveth life"

(2 Corinthians 3:6). That's what most of the New Testament is—letters. The Word and the Spirit must always be one together, not one without the other. The two must agree.

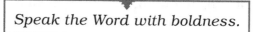

Speak the Word with boldness.

When the disciples prayed, they were filled with the Spirit of God. "Well," you might say, "I've already been baptized with the Spirit of God I've already been filled. I even speak with new tongues!" That may be so, but are you filled with His Spirit and His power and glory now? I know you might have been baptized and filled with the Spirit years ago when you first got saved, but are you filled now? If not, He'll fill you again. To everyone and everybody who opens up to Him, God says, "I will fill them." To everybody who says, "I'm thirsty!" God says, "I'll fill them." Anyone whose cry is, "Lord, I'm longing for Your presence," God says, "I'll fill you." God wants to fill you until you get bold, until timid folks get bold, nervous folks get bold, and scared folks get bold. God says, "I'm gonna fill you until you go tell of the grace and goodness of the Lord."

Speak the Word

You need to speak the Word of God with boldness, not with your feelings, your problems, or situations. You need to set your mind on God's promise and God's Word, and begin to speak the Word of God with boldness. We need not let external circumstances and situations dictate our feelings, behavior, and mind-set. Stop believing what man says and start believing what the Word of God says. What does the Word say?

God's Word declares, "My God shall supply all my needs according to His riches in glory by Christ Jesus...The Lord is my shepherd and I shall not want...By His stripes I am healed...If any man be in Christ he is a new creature, old things have passed away, all things have become new...The earth is the Lord's and the fullness thereof, and they that dwell therein." Speak the Word; speak the Word! If the Word said you shall have whatever you say, then you shall have whatever you say. I dare you to say it. "The Lord is my life and my salvation: whom shall I fear? The Lord is the strength of my life; of whom shall I be afraid? When the wicked, even my enemies and my foes, came upon me to eat up my flesh, they stumbled and fell. Though a host encamped against me, my heart shall not fear...Though wars shall rise against me, in this will I be confident. One thing have I desired of Lord, that will I seek after; that I may dwell in the house of the Lord all the days of my life, to behold the beauty of the Lord and to inquire in His temple. For in the time of trouble He shall hide me in his pavilion: in the secret place of His tabernacle, shall He hide me; He shall set me upon a rock. And now shall my head be lifted up above my enemies around about me: therefore will I offer in His tabernacle sacrifices of joy; I will sing, yea, I will sing praises unto the Lord. Hear O Lord, when I cry with my voice: have mercy also upon me, and answer me. When Thou saidst, Seek ye My face; my heart said unto Thee, Thy face will I seek."

Obviously, if you've read this book up to this point, you have issues in your life that you've been seeking answers about. I pray that what has been said in these pages will be used by the Spirit of God to give you understanding and peace about the present course of your life. If you don't have peace, I pray that because of what you've read, you will feel free to petition and request of the Lord answers for your situation. God has given us all purpose and reason for our own individual lives. We are truly a people of destiny. You need to pursue your destiny by the will and grace of God. But understand and know assuredly that your destiny has a price. It's not without cost. What is the cost? It costs you everything. I close with the words of a late great wise man:

"If you want a thing bad enough to go out and fight for it, to work day and night for it, to give up your time, your peace, and sleep for it. If all that you dream and scheme is about it. If life seems useless and worthless without it. If you'd gladly sweat for it, fret for it, and plan for it. If you lose all your terror of the opposition for it. If you're willing to simply go after the thing you want with all your capacity and tenacity, faith, hope and confidence, and stern personality. If neither cold, famine, poverty, sickness, nor pain of body or mind can keep you from the thing you want. If dogged and determined you besiege and beset it, with the help of God, you will get it!"

GO FORTH!

Thoughts and Reflections

_____
_____
_____
_____
_____
_____
_____
_____
_____
_____
_____
_____
_____
_____
_____
_____
_____
_____
_____
_____
_____
_____
_____
_____
_____
_____

Go Forth!

_____

_____

_____

_____

_____

_____

_____

_____

_____

_____

_____

_____

_____

_____

_____

_____

_____

_____

_____

_____

_____

_____

_____◆

Can You Stand to be Blessed?

The Transformers

*B*ut as many as received Him, to them gave He power to become the sons of God, even to them that believe on His name (John 1:12).

I pray that we as Christians never lose our conviction that God does change lives. We must protect this message. Our God enables us to make the radical changes necessary for fulfilling our purposes and responsibilities. Like the caterpillar that eats and sleeps its way into change, the process occurs gradually, but nonetheless powerfully. Many people who will rock this world are sleeping in the cocoon of obscurity, waiting for their change to come. The Scriptures declare, "...it is high time to awake out of sleep: for now is our salvation nearer than when we believed" (Rom. 13:11).

A memory of my twin sons playing on the floor when they were children tailors the continuity of this text for me. They were playing with a truck, contributing all the sounds of grinding gears and roaring engines. I didn't pay much attention as I began unwinding from the day's stresses and challenges. Distractedly, I glanced down at the floor and noticed that the boys were now running an airplane down an imaginary runway. I asked, "What happened to the truck you were playing with?" They explained, "Daddy, this is a transformer!" I then inquired, "What is a transformer?" Their answer brought me into the Presence of the Lord. They said, "It can be transformed from what it was before into whatever we want it to be!"

Suddenly I realized that God had made the first transformer! He created man from dust. He created him in such a way that, if need be, He could pull a woman out of him without ever having to reach back into the dust. Out of one creative act God transformed the man into a marriage. Then He transformed the marriage

160

into a family, the family into a society, etc. God never had to reach into the ground again because the power to transform was intrinsically placed into man. All types of potential were locked into our spirits before birth. For the Christian, transformation at its optimum is the outworking of the internal. God placed certain things in us that must come out. We house the prophetic power of God. Every word of our personal prophetic destiny is inside us. He has ordained us to be!

> *Before I formed thee in the belly I knew thee; and before thou camest forth out of the womb I sanctified thee, and I ordained thee a prophet unto the nations* (Jeremiah 1:5).

Only when we are weary from trying to unlock our own resources do we come to the Lord, receive Him, and allow Him to release in us the power to become whatever we need to be. Actually, isn't that what we want to know: our purpose? Then we can use the power to become who we really are. Life has chiseled many of us into mere fragments of who we were meant to be. To all who receive Him, Christ gives the power to slip out of who they were forced into being so they can transform into the individual they each were created to be.

Salvation as it relates to destiny is the God-given power to become what God has eternally decreed you were before. "Before what?" you ask; before the foundation of the world. What Christians so often refer to as grace truly is God's divine enablement to accomplish predestined purpose. When the Lord says to Paul, "My grace is sufficient for thee..." (2 Cor. 12:9), He is simply stating that His power is not intimidated by your circumstances. You are empowered by God to reach and accomplish goals that transcend human limitations! It is important that each and every vessel God uses realize that they were able to accomplish what others could not only because God gave them the grace to do so. Problems are not really problems to a person who has the grace to serve in a particular area.

How many times have people walked up to me and said, "I don't see how you can stand this or that." If God has given us the grace to operate in a certain situation, those things do not affect us as they would someone else who does not have the grace to function in that area. Therefore, it is important that we not imitate other people. Assuming that we may be equally talented, we still may not be equally graced. Remember, God always empowers whomever He employs. Ultimately, we must realize that the excellency of our gifts are of God and not of us.

He doesn't need nearly as much of our contributions as we think He does. So it is God who works out the internal destinies of men. He gives us the power to become who we are eternally and internally.

> *Wherefore, my beloved, as ye have always obeyed, not as in my presence only, but now much more in my absence, work out your own salvation with fear and trembling. For it is God which worketh in you both to will and to do of His good pleasure* (Philippians 2:12-13).

Today in the Body of Christ a great deal of emphasis is placed on the process of mentoring. The concept of mentoring is both scriptural and effective; however, as we often do, many of us have gone to extremes. Instead of teaching young men to pursue God, the ultimate Rabbi, they are running amuck looking for a man to pour into them. All men are not mentored as Joshua was—under the firm hand of a strong leader. Some, like Moses, are prepared by the workings of the manifold wisdom of God. This latter group receives mentoring through the carefully orchestrated circumstances that God ordains to accomplish an end result. Regardless of which describes your ascent to greatness, it is still God who "worketh in you both to will and to do." When you understand this, you appreciate the men or the methods God used, but ultimately praise the God whose masterful ability to conduct has crescendoed in the finished product of a man or woman of God.

> *And the Lord said unto Moses, Gather unto Me seventy men of the elders of Israel, whom thou knowest to be the elders of the people, and officers over them; and bring them unto the tabernacle of the congregation, that they may stand there with thee* (Numbers 11:16).

In keeping with this mentoring concept, let's consider Moses' instructions when asked to consecrate elders in Israel. I found it interesting that God told Moses to gather unto Him men whom he knew were elders. God says, "I want you to separate men to be elders who are elders." You can only ordain a man to be what he already is. The insight we need to succeed is the discernment of who is among us. Woe unto the man who is placed into what he is not. Moses was to bring these men into a full circle. In other words, they were to be led into what they already were. Perhaps this will further clarify my point: When the prodigal son was in the "hog pen," it was said, "And when he came to himself..." (Luke 15:17). We are fulfilled only when we are led into being who we were predestined to be. Real success is coming to ourselves.

The thing that gives a man power to arise above his circumstances is his coming to himself. You feel fulfilled when you achieve a sense of belonging through your job, family, or ministry. Have you ever met anyone who left you with a feeling of familiarity-almost as if you had known the person? A sense of bonding comes out of similarities. Likewise, there are certain jobs or ministries that feel comfortable, even if they are tasks you have never done before. If you are discerning, you can feel a sense of belonging in certain situations. However, weary are the legs of a traveler who cannot find his way home. Spiritual wanderings plague the lives of many people who wrestle with discontentment. May God grant you success in finding your way to a sense of wholeness and completion.

Change is a gift from God. It is given to the person who finds himself too far removed from what he feels destiny has ordained for him. There is nothing wrong with being wrong-but there is something wrong with not making the necessary adjustments to get things right! Even within the Christian community, some do not believe in God's ability to change the human heart. This unbelief in God's ability to change causes people to judge others on the basis of their past. Dead issues are periodically revived in the mouths of gossips. Still, the Lord progressively regenerates the mind of His children. Don't assume that real change occurs without struggle and prayer. However, change can be achieved.

God exalted Him to His own right hand as Prince and Savior that He might give repentance and forgiveness of sins to Israel (Acts 5:31 NIV). The Bible calls change repentance. Repentance is God's gift to a struggling heart who wants to find himself. The Lord wants to bring you to a place of safety and shelter. Without the Holy Spirit's help you can search and search and still not find repentance. The Lord will show the place of repentance only to those who hunger and thirst after righteousness. One moment with the Spirit of God can lead you into a place of renewal that, on your own, you would not find or enjoy. I believe it was this kind of grace that made John Newton record, "It was grace that taught my heart to fear and grace my fears relieved. How precious did that grace appear the hour I first believed" (Amazing Grace, early American melody). When God gives you the grace to make changes that you know you couldn't do with your own strength, it becomes precious to you.

For ye know how that afterward, when he would have inherited the blessing, he was rejected: for he found no place of repentance, though he sought it carefully with tears (Hebrews 12:17). Brother Esau sought for the place of repentance and could not secure it. To be transformed is to be changed. If you are not moving into your divine purpose, you desperately need to repent. "Repent" has a strong negative connotation for the person indoctrinated to be-lieve that repentance is a fearful and dangerous action. It is not dangerous. Repentance is the prerequisite of revival. There cannot be revival without prayerful repentance. John the Baptist taught Israel, "Repent ye: for the kingdom of heaven is at hand" (Matt. 3:2). If God wants you to change, it is because He wants you to be prepared for what He desires to do next in your life. Get ready; the best is yet to come.

For whom He did foreknow, He also did predestinate to be conformed to the image of His Son, that He might be the firstborn among many brethren (Romans 8:29).

And be not conformed to this world: but be ye transformed by the renewing of your mind, that ye may prove what is that good, and acceptable, and perfect, will of God (Romans 12:2).

Now let's deal with some real issues! The word conformed in Romans 8:29 is *summormorphoo* (Strong's #4832)[1], which means "to be fashioned like or shaped into the image or the picture" of—in this case—Christ. God has predestined you to shape up into a picture of Christ in the earth. Christ is the firstborn of a huge family of siblings who all bear a striking resemblance to their Father. The shaping of a will, however, requires a visit to the Garden of Gethsemane. Gethsemane literally means *oil press* (Strong's #1068)[2]. God presses the oil of His anointing out of your life through adversity. When you forsake your will in order to be shaped into a clearer picture of Christ, you will see little drops of oil coming out in your walk and work for God. In short, He predestined the pressing in your life that produces the oil. As you are pressed, you gradually conform to the image of your predestined purpose.

In Romans 12:2 we are instructed not to be conformed to this world. Literally, it says we are not to be conformed to the same pattern of this world. The text warns us against submitting to the dictates of the world. We are to avoid using those standards as a pattern for our progress. On a deeper level God is saying, "Do not use the same pattern of the world to measure success or to establish character and values." The term *world* in Greek is *aion* (Strong's #165)[3], which refers to ages. Together these words tell us, "Do not allow the pattern of the times you are in to become the pattern that shapes your inward person."

At this point I can almost hear someone saying, "How do you respond to the preexisting circumstances and conditions that have greatly affected you?" Or, "I am already shaped into something less than what God would want me to be because of the times in which I live or the circumstances in which I grew up." I am glad you asked these things. You see, every aspect of your being that has already been conformed to this age must be transformed! The prefix *trans-* implies movement, as in the words transport, translate, transact, transition, etc. In this light, transform would imply moving the form. On a deeper level it means moving from one form into another, as in the tadpole that is transformed into the frog, and the caterpillar into the butterfly. No matter what has disfigured you, in God is the power to be transformed.

Many individuals in the Body of Christ are persevering without progressing. They wrestle with areas that have been conformed to the world instead of transformed. This is particularly true of us Pentecostals who often emphasize the gifts of the Spirit and exciting services. It is imperative that, while we keep our mode of expression, we understand that transformation doesn't come from inspiration! Many times preachers sit down after ministering a very inspiring sermon feeling that they accomplished more than they actually did. Transformation takes place in the mind.

The Bible teaches that we are to be renewed by the transforming of our minds (see Rom. 12:2; Eph. 4:23). Only the Holy Spirit knows how to renew the mind. The struggle we have inside us is with our self-perception. Generally our perception of ourselves is affected by those around us. Our early opinion of ourselves is deeply affected by the opinions of the authoritative figures in our formative years. If our parents tend to neglect or ignore us, it tears at our self-worth. Eventually, though, we mature to the degree where we can walk in the light of our own self-image, without it being diluted by the contributions of others.

When we experience the new birth, we again go back to the formative years of being deeply impressionable. It's important to be discerning in who we allow to influence us in the early years. Whenever we become intimate with someone, the first thing we should want to know is, "Who do you say that I am?" Our basic need is to be understood by the inner circle of people with whom we walk. However, we must be ready to abort negative, destructive information that doesn't bring us into an accelerated awareness of inner realities and strengths. Jesus was able to ask Peter, "Who do you say that I am?" because He already knew the answer! (See Matthew 16:15). To ask someone to define you without first knowing the answer within yourself is dangerous. When we ask that kind of question, without an inner awareness, we open the door for manipulation. In short, Jesus knew who He was.

The Lord wants to help you realize who you are and what you are graced to do. When you understand that He is the only One who really knows you, then you pursue Him with fierceness and determination. Pursue Him! Listen to what Paul shares at the meeting on Mars Hill.

And hath made of one blood all nations of men for to dwell on all the face of the earth, and hath determined the times before appointed, and the bounds of their habitation; that they should seek the Lord, if haply they might feel after Him, and find Him, though He be not far from every one of us: for in Him we live, and move, and have our being; as certain also of your own poets have said, For we are also His offspring (Acts 17:26-28).

The basic message of this passage is that God has set the bounds on our habitations. He knows who we are and how we are to attain. This knowledge, locked up in the counsel of God's omniscience, is the basis of our pursuit, and it is the release of that knowledge that brings immediate transformation. He knows the hope or the goal of our calling. He is not far removed from us; He reveals Himself to people who seek Him. The finders are the seekers. The door is opened only to the knockers and the gifts are given to the askers! (See Luke 11:9.) Initiation is our responsibility. Whosoever hungers and thirsts shall be filled. Remember, in every crisis He is never far from the seeker!

Transforming truths are brought forth through the birth canal of our diligence in seeking His face. It is while you are in His presence that He utters omniscient insights into your individual purpose and course. Jesus told a woman who had been wrestling with a crippling condition for 18 years that she was not really bound-that in fact she was loosed! Immediately she was transformed by the renewing of her mind. (See Luke 13:11-13.) It is no wonder David said, "In Thy presence is fulness of joy" (Ps. 16:11b). The answer is in the Presence the

172

Presence of God, not man! There is a renewing word that will change your mind about your circumstance. Just when the enemy thinks he has you, transform before his very eyes!

No matter who left his impression upon you, God's Word prevails! The obstacles of past scars can be overcome by present truths. Your deliverance will not start in your circumstances; it will always evolve out of your mentality. As the Word of God waxes greater, the will of men becomes weaker. Paul said in Ephesians 5:26 that Jesus cleanses by the "washing of water by the word." So turn the faucet on high and ease your mind down into the sudsy warm water of profound truth. Gently wash away every limitation and residue of past obstacles and gradually, luxuriously, transform into the refreshed, renewed person you were created to become. Whenever someone tells you what you can't do or be, or what you can't get or attain, then tell them, "I can do all things through Christ who strengthens me! I am a transformer!"

Endnotes:

1. James Strong, *The Exhaustive Concordance of the Bible* (Peabody, MA: Hendrickson Publishers, 1998).

2. Ibid.

3. Ibid.

Other Books
by T. D. Jakes

Additional copies of this book and other
book titles from DESTINY IMAGE are
available at your local bookstore.

Call toll-free: 1-800-722-6774

Send a request for a catalog to:

Destiny Image® **Publishers, Inc.**
P.O. Box 310
Shippensburg, PA 17257-0310

*"Speaking to the Purposes of God for This
Generation and for the Generations to Come."*

**For a complete list of our titles,
visit us at www.destinyimage.com**